i

Just beyond what you think is impossible,
you will find your greatest success.
-   Mike Rodriguez

# Pursuing
# SUCCESS
### Stories That Inspire

Tribute
Publishing
2016

Dedicated to all who are
courageous enough to pursue success.

# Contents

# Prologue

I decided to publish this book because I knew there were others like me who had a story to tell. Others around the world who had faced major challenges they had overcome. Normal people like me and like you that had a story of success to share or who just needed their voice to be heard.

The contributing Authors in this book, some who reside around the world, were brave enough to share their own thoughts, stories, and insights. They did this with the hopes that other people, like you, would find something to take away. Something that would inspire others to make the important changes in their own lives. To understand that what you are going through does not define you, but can certainly refine you. You can do it; however, you must be willing to believe, take action, and start pursuing your greatest purpose in life. I would like to tell you that it is going to be easy, but it is not. I would like to say that there is nothing special about the contributors to this book, but that would also not be true. Yet, it would also be false for you to believe that there is nothing special about you, too. You were created with precision, purpose, and your own unique talents. You were also given the ability to know, act on, and use those talents to become great and strong in your own way. Just know, remember, and most importantly believe this, "I can do all things through Christ, who strengthens me." Philippians 4:13 (*NKJV*). As I always say, "Through faith and action, ALL things are possible."

Now let's get you started on pursuing YOUR success.

"Success is a series of steps taken one at a time. You will slow, you will stop, and you will go backwards, but you must always keep moving forward."

Mike Rodriguez

# Chapter 1

# Three Types of People

When I started my professional career, I was fortunate to be hired by an organization that had established a healthy team culture of performance. Although most people around me were performing, I wasn't a performer and I could feel that I was dragging down the team. I felt terrible. I quickly realized that if I wanted my results to change, then I needed to change. I considered myself capable and smart, I just wasn't working with my true potential. I had developed a bad habit of hanging around with a few individuals who also weren't performing, and I noticed that they complained quite a bit. They had an excuse for everything and their blame, attitudes and belief systems were out of control. I no longer wanted to be part of their group, so I took action to break away from that crowd.

Over the next few years, I would study this phenomenon. As a result, I created categories for stages of people to help monitor my pace and the pace of others that I worked with.

1

Now, years later with decades of experience, I have formalized this study for people like you to easily identify and determine where you rank in your own minds. The mind, of course, is what drives the actions, based on beliefs.

My research has concluded that there are three core types of people in life:

## 1. The Complainers

This group makes up about 22% of people, yet they create the biggest damage. Their bad attitudes and low to no performance not only jeopardize their careers, but they also create negative effects on others in life. These are the people who show up to work (and life) because they have to. They are just living. Something has happened in their lives that has prompted them to lose their focus, their passion, and/or their drive. They aren't happy with some facet of their life, and they let everyone know, either verbally or through their lack of involvement. These people are disappointing in many ways, but primarily because they show up to work, expecting 100% of their paycheck every pay period, while refusing to give 100% effort in return. The core of their foundation is that they don't believe that much is happening or will happen in their lives, but they believe they are owed much. Ironically, they create their own demise through self-destructive behavior.

Complainers are highly deficient in personal accountability and detrimental to the overall health of others they encounter. They come to work late, gossip, conduct personal tasks during business hours, have extended lunch hours, and they leave work early. Nothing is ever their fault and they typically lead a life of blame. Most company cultures are impacted heavily by the complainers, especially when they see more and more complainers develop within the organization. If you have ever worked at a company where people were telling you all the bad things about the employer, peers, product, and everything else they could find wrong, then you were working with complainers. Their disease is highly contagious and their behavior should be addressed quickly with decisive action. Complainers are culture changers, negative impactors, and creators of resistance. Their poor attitudes not only affect their overall life performance, but they will also hold back the progress of everyone they meet if you let them.

The goal isn't to ignore the complainer; the goal is to get them to recognize their unacceptable behavior and to give them the opportunity to take immediate and planned action to correct it. Remember, anyone can brush off someone, but a person with character accepts every challenge to develop others that impact their own lives. Again, if someone isn't willing to improve, then they have already made their decision. When this happens, you must help the person to exit your life. You do this for their own happiness and for your own health and happiness.

The good news is that most complainers are indeed aware that they are complainers. They are normally not called out for their behavior, especially in today's world, so when they are confronted, they will usually respond by either:

a. **getting back on board to win or**
b. **ignoring you and leave you alone**

Either way is a win-win for both of you, but ultimately your goal is to get them to move up to the next level of performance and accountability in life. I have seen many complainers who stay with friends for years because they are never called out for their behavior. I have seen many leave the relationships and take their poor behavior somewhere else. Finally, I have seen a few complainers in my career who take responsibility for their actions and they take action to improve. This group will always need the guidance and mentorship of someone who is tough, fair, caring, and who does not negotiate with mediocrity.

## 2. The Complacent

This group accounts for approximately 68% of people. Complacent people are the ones who show up and do what they are asked to do. They usually won't do any more, unless asked. These are the typical people who have fallen into the daily routines of their lives. They have confused the fact that because they are doing something and they are getting a result, that everything is fine. They live and operate from a perspective that as long as they are comfortable, all in life is okay. This simply isn't true because when most complacent people increase their attitudes and action, we find that they can achieve more out of work and life. The problem is that people in this group are comfortable and they don't want to get uncomfortable, which is a requirement for change. They are indeed capable of producing much more if they can only find a reason to take action. They are missing out on a better quality of life and they aren't giving others the best that either of them deserves. Complacent people should be encouraged and challenged to become all that they are capable of. Help them find their reason to excel and help them grow to the next level.

## 3. The Competitors

This third group is unique and accounts for less than 10% of people, but they have the greatest impact on culture. I have found that almost every person in this group has been a complainer or has been complacent at some point in their life or career. They have experienced the same pains, failures, and personal challenges, yet what makes this group different is that they have decided to overcome these common obstacles to achieve more in life. **They show up to win.**

They have taken personal responsibility and have taken action to make their lives better. They understand that by being a better person, their families, friends and people they work with become better as well.

Competitor's show up to win and they want others to win. They also recognize that winning is a decision. They have purpose, they see the vision, and they take accountability. They have developed the core qualities to become leaders.

However, know that there are two types of competitors:

a. **Reckless Competitor**

These individuals are driven, but they are all about themselves. They will usually do or say whatever is necessary to get the end result to succeed, sometimes at any cost. This group won't usually be part of the team, but they can and sometimes do make the transition to become a:

b. **Balanced Competitor**

People who operate with integrity, passion, teamwork, strategy, and vision. They see the big picture and follow a plan to win.

Regardless of where you are as a person, or where others you know may be in any of these three categories, know that anyone can change if they choose to. They just need to know that they can and that you will support them. This doesn't mean you compromise and lighten up on accountability. This is a living process and you will see the person you know go through different stages, falling into and moving out of each of the three categories, based on their beliefs and attitudes. Your job is to stay engaged and be present in your own life. When people sec that you have their best interest at heart, that you believe in them and that you have high expectations for them, they will surprise you with their willingness to change.

What type of person are you? Why are you in that category? Are you willing to take action to change?

-     By Mike Rodriguez

"Stop planning, stop preparing,
Start taking action.
Success is waiting for YOU!"
Mike Rodriguez

# Chapter 2

# A Dream Fulfilled
By Martin Chase

**Speak Over Yourself**

Like most kids, I always dreamed of taking care of my mother and being an NFL superstar. I'd run around the house and tell my mother my plans of playing in the NFL and taking care of her and my grandmother. They were my two favorite ladies (and still are). My grandmother would smile when I'd brag about the "glittery" dress I would buy her and the Cadillacs that I'd get for her and my mother. That dream stuck with me as I grew older.

**Have a Strong Foundation**

Growing up in a single-parent home, I always thought my mother and I were rich. Misfortunes like seeing my mom walk to work while I walked to school because her car wouldn't start, or eating ramen noodles for dinner, never made me feel like we were poor. My mother always made sure that I was fed and clothed, that the lights were on, and that we had running water. All of our needs were met. Looking back, my mom was the real superwoman. She never once let me worry about anything. There were days I would look in her eyes and could see how tired she was from

9

working hours on end only to come home and take care of me. It was at home that I first learned the true definitions of perseverance, dedication, and hard work.

Throughout my childhood, I took the examples set by my mother and incorporated them with my love of football. It wasn't until I began playing football at Lawton Eisenhower High School in Lawton, Oklahoma, that I began to realize all that I dreamed could really come true. I had the best coach in all of Oklahoma, if not the country. Coach Tim Reynolds was a tough coach, especially with me. Growing up I always had a tough time when it came to football on account of my size. There were times I'd have to bring my birth certificate to prove my age. I think all of my coaches saw potential in me, but Coach Reynolds made it his mission to make sure I saw the potential in myself. One day he got in my face and told me, "Son, if you want to be the best, you're gonna have to act like it. And every day that you come on this field you're gonna have to show yourself, not me, not none of these guys around you, but yourself of how bad you wanna be the best." From that day on he lit a fire in me that I use as my motivation every day of my life.

**It's the Little Things**
When Coach Reynolds left LEHS, a new coach came by the name of Coach Stiles. Coach Stiles taught me to pay attention to the details. Every little detail matters and makes a difference. It was paying attention to the details that made me a better player. Although I knew I was bigger and stronger than most, I also knew the day would come when I

would meet my Goliath, and it would be my ability to pay attention to the details that would allow me to conquer my Goliath. I took everything I was learning and applied it daily. Finally, my hard work paid off and I got a letter from the University of Oklahoma (among others). I was born and raised a Boomer Sooner. It was never a question of where I'd go to college.

## Preparing for the Dream

Reflecting back on my life, I made a lot of sacrifices to make sure I could focus on the prize. As a young teen, I didn't hang out with friends, attend wild parties, or even attend my high school prom. I had a one-track mind and that track was going to lead me to the NFL. You don't know the exact day your dreams will come true. You just know you've done everything you can to make sure that when your dream does come true, you are as prepared as you can be. NFL scouts began showing up to my college games and practices. I was being asked questions about my life and family. Coaches began working with me even harder. I was working out, eating right, and even dropped my classes for the college semester to make sure I had no distractions. The dream was within my grasp and I had to be ready.

## A Dream Fulfilled

It was a Saturday morning; I watched with butterflies in my stomach as day two of the NFL draft started. The night before had been stressful. I'd expected to be picked up in the $3^{rd}$ round, but that didn't happen. With bated breath, the $5^{th}$ round was starting and the first name was called, "Martin

Chase, Lawton, Oklahoma…." Tears ran down my face. The wait was over. My home phone rang. It was the coaching staff of the Baltimore Ravens. "Are you ready to be a Raven?" Ozzie Newsome, the Ravens General Manager, asked. "Yes sir!" I exclaimed. "Alright, we'll get you with our secretary and get your flight arranged." And just like that, I went from being an OU Boomer Sooner to a Baltimore Raven in the NFL.

I spent eight years in the NFL, had a lot of experiences, and learned a lot of lessons. With God and hard work, my dreams came true. My grandmother went to heaven before I was able to get her that glittery dress, but I did get my mom a Cadillac and she can be spotted driving around in it to this day. Looking back over my journey, I can say I lived my dream and accomplished what I always wanted to accomplish. You can do the same. I knew at a young age what I wanted to do. It was as a young man that I really saw my dream as more than just a dream, but as a reality.

**The Game Plan**
Is there really a game plan? I think so. You have to know what you want. You can't properly prepare for a dream fulfilled if you don't know what your dream is. Oftentimes, people just say what they want, or what they wish they had, but no real game plan of how to get it. Once you clearly define your desires and passions then examine how they line up with your wants and needs, you're ready to begin building your game plan. Some say protect your dream by telling only a select few what you want to do. I totally disagree. I say tell

EVERYONE. You need to tell anyone who will listen what your dreams are and for good reason:

1. Telling people what your dreams are allows you to see their reactions and know off the bat who is likely to support you and who is likely to want to discourage you. You can't protect yourself from what you don't know. Those who give off the vibe of not supporting your dreams are the ones who will fuel your fire, but also the ones you know to stay away from.

2. You never know if the person you are sharing your dream with will have a connection that can help you achieve your dream. That person who you've confided in could hold the key to helping you achieve your dream that much faster.

3. Sharing your dream holds you accountable. When I say this, I mean that you are more likely to work ten times harder to see your dream come to fruition because you have so many eyes on you.

So now you've told the world your dream. You know what you want to do and why you want to do it. Next, it's time to establish a plan of execution. Research, research, research. Most likely there is someone doing, has done, or tried to do what you are doing. Finding out what worked for them and what didn't can save you a lot of headache.

Create a list of actions. What can you do daily, weekly, monthly, etc. that will prepare you for your dream to be fulfilled? The smallest step towards a goal is better than no step at all. Set realistic goals. If you set crazy highly-involved and complex goals right off the top, you're setting yourself up for failure. I knew I wanted to play in the NFL, so I played football every single day. It was fun for me, but also preparing me. Don't forget to have fun while you're working towards your dream. Your dream is supposed to be fun for you, that's why you chose it in the first place. It's something you're good at. It's something you enjoy.

Set deadlines. Knowing exactly when you want to have a specific goal accomplished gives you some structure. Without deadlines, you end up spending unnecessary amounts of time on a task. You need to know what you want to do, how you want to do it, and roughly how long it should take you to do it. This gives structure to your list of goals.

Keep track of your accomplishments. Making a checklist of what you need to do and checking things off as you accomplish them gives a sense of satisfaction. You can actually see your progress, which will encourage you to challenge yourself to do even more. If you hit a roadblock while trying to work on a specific goal, don't become frustrated. Sometimes it will become necessary to reevaluate your plan. Don't change the desired outcome; just adjust the path to get there. This may happen several times during your journey. I hit a few roadblocks on my road to the NFL, but I found a detour and persevered. Sometimes you have to take a timeout and regroup. Sit quietly and visualize yourself living your dream. Take note of the peace and happiness you feel in that moment of your dream fulfilled. Once you've refocused, go back to attacking your goals with a renewed mind and determination. Sometimes we just have to remind ourselves of the awesome outcome awaiting us if we just stay focused. Becoming discouraged and wallowing in that moment for too long can be dangerous and result in a major setback, if not total failure. The mind will be the battleground while trying to obtain your goals even when you achieve them. There will be a small voice that will sneak up and whisper in your ear from time to time, but if you have on your mental armor you will quickly tackle any negative thoughts.

Remember to focus. There are many different ways to accomplish one thing. You have to find what works best for you and focus on that. Once you've exhausted that option, then you can explore another option, but trying to test several different options at once will overwhelm, exhaust, and discourage you. Believe that you know what you are doing and that it is best for the current situation until proven otherwise.

During all of this hard work remember to reward yourself. You're setting goals, creating lists, and getting the job done, so why not celebrate you and your accomplishments? This allows you to hit the reset button, take a step back, and applaud yourself on a job well done.

Rank your goals. What seems to be the most immediately meaningful goal could fall 2$^{nd}$ to another goal. Once you've listed the goals, rank them in order of easiest to hardest to begin accomplishing them. As you work through your list, you are creating a workflow allowing you to become more and more comfortable with how to tackle them.

Identify your obstacles upfront. Knowing the difficulties you are facing mentally prepares you so there are no surprises. Maybe you're working in corporate America while trying to start your own business. Knowing you can't quit your job today, you have to create an alternative. Setting a schedule will help greatly with keeping you on track and underwhelmed. The reality is that there will be obstacles and properly preparing equals success.

Another big key is learning to be a self-motivator. Remember, you're working on YOUR dream. There are those who will be happy for you, but they will not necessarily be the ones making the sacrifice with you. There will come those late nights or holidays when time with friends and family will be cut short because you need to meet personal and professional deadlines. You will want to make excuses to justify procrastinating on your to-do list. You will tell yourself to throw in the towel and do things another day. DON'T! When you want to throw in the towel and pull the plug on the whole thing, you need to be able to look at yourself in the mirror and be your own Coach Reynolds, giving yourself a pep talk and pushing yourself forward.

The process of achieving your dream will become a relationship. You will have days when you love it and days when you hate it, just like your relationship with your significant other. There will be good days and bad days, but through it all you love them and wouldn't be with anyone else. That's the relationship you must have with achieving your dreams. I remember there were days when my body was sore, I didn't feel like being yelled at by my coaches, and I wanted to go home and just lay on the sofa or hang out with my friends, but I knew that my love for football and the NFL was greater than all of it and although my body hurt, it was a pain I came to enjoy. Although I wanted to hang out with my friends, I enjoyed being able to take care of my mom. My hard work allowed me to be able to do those things and I loved that living my dream afforded me the ability to do those things.

Lastly, remember this will be a trying process. Believe in yourself. Don't compromise yourself. There are no shortcuts. Lao Tzu said it best, "A journey of a thousand miles begins with a single step." Start your journey today. Take that first step today. You will encounter numerous roadblocks along your journey. Don't let negativity fester. Never give up. Stay focused and stay inspired.

It's been eight years since I played in the NFL. My dream was fulfilled and now I am moving on to my next dream. I am starting on page one of my newest journey. I am sharing my plan. Making my list. Researching those who came before me. I am starting a new journey with new goals. I know the process, but this is a new path. The great thing about life is that we can have more than one dream and we can achieve more than one dream. How many exactly is up to us. I know I am excited for the new path, for the ups and downs that will come with it. I've fallen in love with the process of fulfilling my dreams. I've fallen in love with the late nights and sacrifices. I love it all because I know the feeling of a dream fulfilled and I am so excited to experience it again.

I invite you to join me as I venture on my new path of becoming a motivational speaker and encouragement coach. I've been posting daily motivational texts on my social media pages. I've been connecting with professionals in the field, sharing my dream on social media, and attending different seminars in the U.S. I've even had business cards made and challenged myself to hand out a few each day. We all have dreams and we all need to keep each other lifted with encouragement. I believe in you. Take advantage of each day. Never give up.

- Martin Chase

"The Encouragement Coach"

## About the Author – Martin Chase

Throughout his life Martin Chase has achieved success through hard work, discipline, a positive attitude, and self-motivation. As a youth, he excelled at sports and received a scholarship to play football at The University of Oklahoma. At the University of Oklahoma Martin was the Sooner's Football Captain in 1996 and 1997. In 1998 Martin was drafted in the 5th round by The Baltimore Ravens to play professional football. Martin played in the NFL for 8 years, playing for the Baltimore Ravens, the New Orleans Saints, the Washington Redskins, the New York Giants and the Jacksonville Jaguars.

Since retiring from the NFL, Martin has been an active partner in multiple businesses. He is a professional motivational speaker, talking at schools, organizations, and businesses. Martin's goal as a motivational speaker is to inspire and encourage people to feel better about themselves and achieve their dreams, just as he did by beating the odds to become an NFL Player. Martin inspires people on both an emotional and mental level to help them create positive personal change in their lives.

Connect with Martin Chase:

Facebook:
www.facebook.com/martinchaseencouragementcoach
LinkedIn:
www.linkedin.com/in/martinchase
Instagram:
mcencouragementcoach

# Chapter 2 – A Dream Fulfilled

"You have to know what you want.
You can't properly prepare for a dream fulfilled
if you don't know what your dream is."
- Martin Chase

# Chapter 3 – Marriage: An Adventure in Love

# Chapter 3

# Marriage: An Adventure in Love
By Shane Adamson

As a marriage counselor, I have walked alongside the very personal and intimate path of marital challenges and successes. This experience has given me the precious experience of witnessing what works and what does not work in building a loving and happy marriage. Please trust me to be your tour guide in hopes of offering you a clear map for navigating the awesome adventure of love and marriage. I will start with simple tips that fall under the category of marriage enrichment and close with some tips for more difficult marital challenges. Before getting too deep, let me lighten the mood by looking at how we come to understand love and marriage.

Can you remember what you thought about marriage as a kid? Let me help you remember. Here are some random thoughts about love and marriage from kids:

"Marriage is when you get to keep your girl and don't have to give her back to her parents!"    -Eric, 6

# Chapter 3 – Marriage: An Adventure in Love

"No one is sure why love happens, but I heard it has something to do with how you smell ... That's why perfume and deodorant are so popular."     -Mae, age 9

"It isn't always just how you look.  Look at me.  I'm handsome like anything and I haven't got anybody to marry me yet."     -Brian, age 7

"One of you should know how to write a check.  Because, even if you have tons of love, there is still going to be a lot of bills."     -Ava, age 8

"I know one reason that kissing was created. It makes you feel warm all over, and they didn't always have electric heat or fireplaces or even stoves in their houses."     -Gina, age 8

I start with kids' view of love and marriage because the science of love in social science is called "attachment theory." Our understanding of love and marriage starts at an early age. I will explain in a basic way how love and attachment are related. Our early life experiences in family life, influence how we love and choose our spouse, as well as how we act in marriage life. Most people dream about finding a best friend, a lover, a safe person, a fun person to do marriage life. It is important to recognize where our preferences develop and why we choose that "significant someone" to marry. Also, once we marry, how deeply we attach is often influenced by our early attachment experiences with parents, family, and others.

In order to better understand how you learn about love, I want you to imagine that you are observing the drop-off process at a preschool for 4-year-old children. For some children, this is the first time a child will be separated from their parent(s) for an extended period of time. Children who are securely attached to their parents most often give their mom or dad a hug and dart into the playground. These children feel secure because they have received lots of love and attention, and trust their parents are leaving them in a safe place. On the other hand, children who have sporadic messages of love or perhaps been left in random or awkward places are going to display more fearful and anxious behaviors. These children are often seen clinging to their parent's leg and are sometimes tearful, as they fear being left alone with strangers. There are also some children who have received love, attention, and safe childcare placements, but the unique personality of the child and/or life experiences result in strong feelings of anxiety and insecurity when left alone. In general, children in loving and secure families are able to separate without too much fear or anxiety.

Your early life experience with your parents is your first understanding of what love and bonding with others feels like. The accumulation of loving messages from your parents become literal confidence boosters as you mature toward the time when you will leave your family home. Of course, there are other experiences that strengthen and mature you, such as sports, school, religion, and friendships. Your parent(s) love combined with your early life experiences shape your character, develop your personality, and build your confidence in significant ways. Social science research tells us that the strength of your attachment to your parents and the security that comes from being deeply loved, mentored, and parented, is a paramount positive influence for you as a young adult to launch into adulthood with a healthy amount of self-esteem and security. It also prepares you for the marriage relationship.

There are so many challenges that occur during childhood. Some of these experiences may include being bullied, failing a class, feeling left out, falling in love, and being rejected by someone you love. Ideally, a parent can be at these crucial crossroads to walk alongside their son or daughter to a place of safety and healing. Parents do the best they can, but sometimes children suffer alone through some of these life-challenges. Some parents are disengaged from their children or are just too consumed with work. Other parents can be the opposite of disengaged and be enmeshed in their children. These parents are often called "helicopter parents," as they tend to hover over their children even into adulthood. Divorce is another common issue that leads to a breakdown in family leadership, limits time between parent and child, and messes with family traditions that at one time created family togetherness. Children of divorce can have a distrust of marriage being a happy experience due to being caught in the crossfire of their parents' marital troubles. It is important to note that as we reach adulthood, we each have some hurts, habits, and hang-ups due to all of these accumulated life challenges. Despite all of our personal baggage, social research tells us that a majority of adults choose to marry at least once in their life.

Let's talk more about the adventure of love that is unique to marriage life. Think about how the power of love can lead each of us to take big risks! Marriage happens when two naïve people, who come from very different family backgrounds, who have unique personalities, habits, and interests, fall in love and decide to say, "YES I DO... I want to live with you... I choose to do life together with you." You can only imagine that there will be some difficulty and conflict in this unique adventure called marriage.

**Tip 1: Remember that marriage has seasons similar to winter, spring, summer and fall.**

I believe courtship can best be likened to spring. There is so much excitement in finding someone you are attracted to and this person is interested in you, too! Your youthful optimism leads to quick growth in love, dreams, and goals to be shared together. You often stay up late talking together. You cannot get enough of this new person you love. Honeymoon and early marriage are likened to summer. You experience the warm feelings of passion and sexual intimacy. The future feels as bright as the summer sun as you run hand-in-hand into this new life adventure "as a couple!"

As a marriage counselor, many couples come to see me in the fall or winter of their marriage. The coldness in the relationship is felt as couples rarely sit close in the first session. After brief introductions, the blame fest starts. Each has a story to tell, and both are hurting due to a complex pattern of conflict that neither seems to be able to find a permanent solution. Underneath all the content of the conflict, I can hear and sense the underlying thoughts and questions: Does my partner really care about me? Will he stop giving me the silent treatment? Will she stop nagging me? Will we be able to get back to that loving feeling we both enjoyed in the beginning? I am afraid we are deeply stuck! It feels more like a roommate relationship, not a marriage relationship! Both are hurt and scared. Both want their partner to have a personality makeover and many come to counseling hoping I can validate their pain and fix the problem—their partner. Some enter counseling with a more reasonable perspective: that their marital problems are most likely a mutually created issue and it will require work and effort by both parties to repair and heal the marriage.

To the reader of this chapter, if you happen to be in a fall or winter season of your marriage, there is still hope. Most often, some unresolved hurt lingers and one or both of you are neglecting your marriage. I encourage you to go to your spouse and say something like this: "I am feeling sad and lonely about our marriage. I miss the feeling of love that comes when we are connected. I am willing to do my part of listening to your perspective. I hope you can also hear my perspective. Most important, let's both commit to bringing our best selves to the marriage." It works best when both put in the effort, but sometimes I have watched one person revive an emotionally starved marriage. As you patiently nurture your marriage over time, a new marriage season can begin to awaken. The cold feelings can thaw out, spring can bloom fresh new feelings, and summer can warm your interactions and brighten your perspective toward your spouse. Marriage life can be pleasantly warm again.

It is important to clarify that some couples can suffer through long seasons of winter. One spouse can suffer from a lifelong physical ailment or injury, a mental health challenge can be chronic, a bankruptcy can cripple hope, and an affair can bring distance and distrust for many years. When longer trials occur in your marriage, it becomes a real test of character. You will need an added measure of patience and faith to endure long, cold marriage winters. Remember your future is as bright as your faith. You can pray and feel yourself strengthened. You can reach to a friend and feel supported. It was once said, "If you find yourself in hell…keep walking." My experience tells me that couples who endure even the really long and cold winters of marriage will get a deep sense of accomplishment of doing a "really hard thing" as they feel the warmth of summer, which may include the passion of early marriage and the maturity of a shared history. If the complexity of the problems persist and are heavier than what you can realistically bear, reach out for professional help. Even a troubled marriage is worth fighting for.

## Tip 2: The 2 Minute Miracle.

I need to give credit for this tip to my awesome wife. I had a bad habit of not managing my mornings well and scrambling to find my keys or wallet before leaving the house. My frantic personality created an uncomfortable feeling of tension in the house just before I left home. My return home was not much better. I often would come home and go to the fridge, mail, computer or TV. This resulted in my wife feeling like just another "thing" in my life. She wanted something different. She wanted to feel "high priority" to me. She reminded me that she was the most important thing in the house and when I come home, she expects me to find her, hug her, and kiss her as my FIRST act as I enter the home. My wife's advice eventually impacted our mornings and evenings in a miraculous way. I decided to call this the 2-minute miracle as it was a short time ritual, but resulted in her feeling important as well as strengthened our marriage.

Here is a description of the two-minute miracle in a nutshell:

Make the two minutes **before you leave** and the two minutes **after you reunite** focused on emotionally connecting with your spouse. Before leaving the house, the husband embraces his wife in a warm hug and says, "I am going to miss you today. What do you have on your agenda today?" He listens and may ask something such as, "Is there anything I can do for you today?" He then gives her a good-bye kiss. Hint: a seven-second kiss once in a while, feels much different than a one-second peck. He leaves. It only takes two minutes, but the lingering love-connection will be worth the two-minute investment in the marriage. The *2 Minute Miracle* in the evening looks something like this: Wife hears her husband enter the home. She drops what she is doing to greet her husband. As the husband enters, he avoids getting distracted and goes to his wife. They find each other and greet each other with a warm welcome hug and kiss. They both visit for a couple minutes about one another's day.

Over the years, our two-minute miracle has evolved from a short peck and hug to sitting somewhere together to visit longer and decompress from the day's activities. If you feel disconnected in your marriage, start with the two-minute miracle then let it evolve into something meaningful for your marriage.

## Tip 3: Remember that marriage communication problems may really be a heart problem.

This may sound like an unusual tip, but let me explain. When couples call me on the phone to schedule a couple's session, it is very common for the caller to say, "We have major communication problems." Once we start the first counseling session, I carefully tune-in to each spouse as they unload their complaints about the marriage. Clarity reveals that both spouses oftentimes hold a combination of many toxic feelings such as resentment, anger, and bitterness in their heart especially around certain hurtful events in their marriage. When they try to talk about even simple things, these unresolved negative emotions leak out on one another, which leads to tension and conflict. These couples can communicate well with friends and colleagues, but with their spouse, they really do have a hard-heart problem. Some marital hurts have not been fully addressed or healed, which results in bitterness and resentment lingering in one or both of their hearts. Thus, resentment and hurt stuck in the heart becomes the main problem.

The path of healing for these couples often happens in three levels of change. I learned about the concept of "levels of change" from a great article entitled, "Change Yourself, Change Your Marriage," by Doug Abbot. The first level of change is a "change in behavior." A key behavioral shift in the marriage is when the withdrawer in the relationship stops shutting down emotionally and starts to cooperate in important conversations. In most marriages, husbands tend to withdraw from heavy marital talks, especially emotionally-charged conversations. The husband feels he is avoiding fighting and thus, helping the marriage. The wife views his avoidant behavior as unhelpful and strongly complains that important issues rarely seem to get resolved. For him to stay in important conversations, the pursuer, (most often the wife) needs to soften her intensity. She may not realize her tone comes across as blaming and intense. As she softens her approach, he will feel safer to stay present in the hard conversations. Once he stops withdrawing and she softens, the relationship atmosphere is safer. The connection and communication will then become easier. Sometimes this dynamic is so complex it takes a professional to slow down the couple's quick pattern of disconnection and develop new habits that result in more understanding. Once each spouse feels understood, connection grows and other behaviors like acts of service, gifts, date nights, and other gestures of love, will be more meaningful and effective.

The second level of change is a "change in attitude." I describe this attitude change as seeing your partner with a new set of eyes. Have you ever held a pebble up close to your eye? If you have done this, the pebble looks like a boulder. Similarly, when you over focus on your spouse's weaknesses, they become boulder issues. Each spouse needs to shift their focus more on the strengths and those things that brought them together. Another helpful tip is the approach you take in asking for what you need. If your spouse is doing something that hurts or bugs you, ask your spouse in a respectful way, "Are you open to some feedback?" It is important that your spouse is "ready" or your feedback will be met with defensiveness. If your spouse is open, provide feedback in a respectful manner, such as, "It would mean a lot to me if you could do more of _____." Another way of asking respectfully is: "I would appreciate it if you would do less _____." You also need to be humble and ready to receive feedback that your spouse will have for you. In short, look for the positive attributes in your spouse, and when needed, ask to give your spouse feedback. Ensure your feedback is presented in a respectful manner. Spouses need to teach one another how to live together in love and peace.

The third level of change is called a "softening of hearts." I believe that spirituality is a key resource that all people can access to experience a "softening" of one's heart in marriage. I am a Christian and derive much of my spiritual health and development through faith practices and personal worship rituals. As a professional counselor that serves the general public, I need to make room in the counseling office for a broader view of spirituality. I encourage those who do not belong to a religion to consider that inner-voice that inspires them to be altruistic and persuades them to do good. I seek to help clients to connect with the spiritual part of themselves.

I believe that inner-voice is the Holy Spirit and it desires to be altruistic, kind, and loving, and to seek the happiness of marriage, family, and our neighbor. Our ego is in opposition to our conscience (spiritual self) and its primary desire is to be selfish. When a person is hard-hearted in marriage, he/she will ignore the spirit's promptings and thus, be slow to respond to the needs of their spouse. In contrast, a spiritually in-tune person is soft-hearted toward their spouse, which results in being quick to say sorry, serving one's spouse without prompting, and naturally looking for ways to express love and meet their spouse's needs. In short, changes in both behavior and attitude toward one's spouse can come more quickly and naturally for someone who can listen and follow the spirit's promptings. The spirit softens hearts in a way that is critically important for individuals and marriage to grow.

A good example of this softening of the heart can be seen in the movie **Fireproof**, the top-selling independent film from 2008. For those who have not seen the movie, I will give you a short summary: Caleb is a firefighter who becomes addicted to internet pornography and over time becomes more selfish. The wife discovers his secret pornography use as well as his intention to spend the family savings on a boat. She is upset and feels betrayed. The husband's reaction to being discovered is not remorseful or penitent; instead, he becomes angry at her over-reactiveness and at the worst point, he even gets physically aggressive with her. She distances herself from him and it looks as if she will end the marriage. She works as a hospital administrator and a doctor she works with is showing her more warmth while her husband is being cold and mean. The estranged husband goes to his father for advice. His father introduces his son to the Love Dare – a daily devotional to save a troubled marriage.

The husband is desperate and not wanting to lose his wife, he starts the Love Dare. The daily devotional consists of Bible verses offering insights about the many aspects of love and a daily new challenge to love more fully and deeply. Here are some examples: Day 1 – Love is Patient; Day 2 – Love is Kind; later in the love dare, you are challenged to NOT say anything negative to your spouse for one full day. Each day offers about 3-4 paragraphs and a daily challenge. In the movie, the wife is slow to respond to Caleb's love dare gestures as she is slow to trust that these behaviors are authentic nor will they be long lasting. In the climax of the movie, Catherine learns that Caleb used the family savings to pay for her mother's medical bills and not the boat. This was the first sign that their marital love may be salvaged. She also learns the doctor, who had been flirting with her, was married, and she became less trusting of his intentions toward her. The movie ends as Caleb and Catherine recommit their love through a vow renewal.

I encourage the reader when faced with major marital or life challenges, to consider these three levels of change: 1 – change of behavior, 2 – change in attitude, and 3 – accessing your spiritual resources for strength and guidance. The heaviness and complexity of the problems facing many couples today require crucial character strengths of kindness, love, patience, and the ability to suffer through problems that do not pass quickly. As each spouse softens their heart, the marriage becomes a soft and safe place to land from the stressors of life. Two spouses who each have tender and soft hearts for one another have the best prognosis for marital success.

## Tip 4: Adversity can refine and strengthen YOU and YOUR MARRIAGE.

I am going to be vulnerable and authentic by closing this chapter with a personal story. It is a hard and personal story to tell, but an important one, as it has been a trial that has matured me into a better husband, father, and counselor. As a counselor, I teach my clients a favorite thought by Brene Brown "The bravest thing we ever do is own our life story." I am still in the trial of this marital challenge and "owning my story," but feel I am far enough along that I can offer some principles for enduring very hard marital challenges.

Here it is: My paramount life adversity is feeling deeply betrayed when my wife chose to leave the practice of our family faith of Mormonism. The reason for this being such a major loss is that marriage in the temple to a Mormon is considered to be the pinnacle life experience in your life path. It is deeper than an experience; a temple marriage is a sacred ordinance called a "sealing," meaning that our marriage and family is sealed through God's power for eternity, not "until death do us part." When Wendy chose to walk away from being part of the Mormon faith, it was much deeper than stopping attending church. From Wendy's point of view, she grew up in a controlling environment. She then married a strong Mormon who she felt was rigid in the way he practiced religion. She left as a way to heal her issues with "control."

Over the next three years, I would suffer and learn through many challenging events. During this time of adversity, we both endured a four-month separation, a near divorce, family drama, and struggles over how to co-parent without a unified value system. This adversity brought me to my knees. With God's help and a social support network, I gradually transformed from being a victim to a survivor of an extreme life adversity. I still have my moments of fear, loneliness, bitterness, and betrayal. The key is, these are only moments, not days, and I have tools to shift from pain into peace and acceptance. Here are some of the key areas of growth that helped me endure well.

## Growing out of fear into faith.

Thomas Monson is the current prophet for the Church of Jesus Christ of Latter Day Saints during my life adversity 2010 to present. My favorite quote he said is: "Your future is as bright as your faith." The first year after Wendy left the church, I primarily lived in fear. Many Sundays became battleground days where my pain of bitterness surfaced and I became reactive over the slightest issues. Over time, I realized I was not trusting that God is mindful of Wendy, myself, and our children. As I matured and practiced living in faith, my daily affirmation has been, "I can be at peace because I have faith that God has got this."

## Growing out of loss and loneliness into gratitude and connection.

I typically seek solutions to my personal problems in the solitude of study and prayer. I continued with this practice, but soon realized this was too big to heal alone. I reached out to others who had spouses leave the faith, I joined a support group, I did counseling, and I shared my story with safe people. A good friend said, "Don't let religion get in the way of your marriage." This timely advice shifted my focus to loving Wendy unconditionally. Couple prayer was a trigger for both of us in different ways. We decided for a period of time to do a gratitude list as a nightly ritual. This shifted my perspective to what I have instead of what I have lost. Gratitude and connection with others minimized my feelings of loss and loneliness. I no longer suffer silently and I can see the abundance of my life more clearly.

## Growing out of shame and bitterness into love and acceptance.

In the beginning of this trial, Sundays felt like I was dumped into a washing machine where instead of detergent, feelings of bitterness and shame washed over me much of the day, especially at church. Mormon culture is highly family-focused. For many months, I was either alone or felt like a single father with a broken family, as it was common to have one or none of my three children beside me. I felt flawed, like a misfit in my congregation, and even worse, a marriage and family counselor that couldn't use his degree to keep his family together. Feelings of toxic shame lead me to shrink in confidence. Bitterness and loss resulted in my having outbursts of passive-aggressive behaviors toward my wife. I was face-down in the arena of life and I was discouraged and angry.

I read Brene Brown's books on shame. I prayed for love and patience. I stopped sitting in the back row of the chapel and sat in the middle or even the front. I volunteered for opportunities to serve. I accepted that my wife needed a break from organized religion to heal her personal and complicated wounds around control. I asked her to tell me about her pain. It was so hard to hear her pain and even harder to hear ways I was part of her trauma around religion. Instead of being defensive or venting my pain, I leaned in to understand her pain. I sincerely apologized. Overtime, we became a safe place for one another emotionally.

I admitted to her that I still pray that she will come back to the faith we started our marriage doing, but hopefully practice it in a safer way for her. She smiled and said to me, "I can't say I will or I won't return, but I need you to love me no matter what I choose." I agreed to love her no matter what. Our love is an ointment for both of our pain. Understanding both of us are in pain is a crucial insight to remember. We both continue to heal and grow in love as we struggle to navigate a mixed-faith marriage. We healed enough that we both call our marriage "a soft-place to land" at the end of a hard day. Once we both felt the security and sincerity of our unconditional love, we both agreed to do a vow renewal for our 20th wedding anniversary.

Shane's Vow Renewal to Wendy Jones Adamson. South Padre Island, June 15, 2013

"My dearest Wendy, you are my awesome wife, my personal cheerleader, my soft place to fall, my co-leader of our family, and my best friend. 20 years ago, we made a pledge before God and to one another and to all those we hold dear to be committed to one another and love one another for life.

Today I am honored and feel so fortunate to renew my commitment of love to you. This ceremony on this beautiful beach symbolizes a new marriage and beautiful bright future together. I feel a great sense of accomplishment that we have grown stronger through the adversities of life. I feel so blessed to have YOU in my life. You are still the best part of each day. You still have the power to surprise me with your love and thoughtful ways. You make my life complete and I am a better person because of you. And it is my heart's prayer that we can enjoy more accomplishments, adventures, grandchildren, and a golden retirement living out our dreams together. Thank you for saying YES 20 years ago and THANKS for SAYING YES AGAIN today. Thank you for being the most special part of my world. I promise to always stand by you as your loving and devoted husband and give you the very best of me. I love you with all my heart…and believe the best is yet to be." Love, Shane

Wendy's Vow Renewal to Shane Adamson. South Padre Island, June 15, 2013

"20 years ago we committed our lives to each other. The road was sure and exciting. Our marital road has twisted and turned in ways neither of us could have imagined. Look how much we have grown and changed in the process. I have learned that life is not a cookie cutter path. Each person's journey is different…I am so glad our journey can be together. Thank you for giving us three beautiful children that make life such an adventure. I feel the love we have is stronger than ever. I vow to give you all of my heart—to put you and God first in my life. Shane, I treasure you and look forward to growing old with you, my very best friend. I welcome the hopes, dreams, challenges we will face together. Thank you for loving and valuing me for who I am. I will love and cherish you with all of my heart." Love, Wendy

Marriage is an adventure where we learn how to love more deeply and unconditionally. After Wendy and my vow renewal, I searched for a way to include a "vow renewal" type experience for couples attending our "Hold Me Tight Marriage Workshop." I found what I was looking for from the Native American Anasazi tribe. The Anasazi Indians have a tradition called the "Blanket Stepping Ceremony."

At our marriage workshop on the final day activity, we lie down two blankets. One blanket is older, tattered, worn and faded in color. The other blanket is more vibrant in color and texture. We have prepared each couple in advance by asking them to reflect on things they desire to leave behind (selfishness, bitterness, pride). We also encourage couples to reflect on the insights around new practices they desire to make a part of their new marriage (promises, date nights, listening). Couples each take a turn doing this pinnacle workshop experience – a blanket stepping ceremony. The couple holds hands and stands on the old blanket. In turn, each expresses what he/she plans to leave behind. This symbolizes letting go of the "old marriage habits." Next, each couple steps onto the colorful vibrant blanket symbolizing a "new beginning" marriage. Tears often come as each spouse sincerely renews their love and commitments to one another. The feeling of hope is so bright it can be felt by all who watch the special and sacred vow renewal.

No matter where your marriage is today, I am here to echo Robert Browning's poetic phrase, "Grow old along with me; the best is yet to be!" I also enjoy Robert Karen's description of marital love when he said, "In love, you don't have to be rich or smart or talented or funny. You just have to be there." Most distress in the marriage relationship comes when you feel your spouse is not responding to your reaches for connection. I encourage you to let go of habits that hurt your marriage and develop those habits that will allow love to grow. Commit to bring your best self to the marriage so you both can more fully enjoy this adventure called marriage! Remember love is the greatest of all gifts life has to offer and marriage is a special relationship where we can experience love more fully and deeply. May God bless you to grow in love through this awesome adventure called marriage.

-    Shane Adamson

## About the Author – Shane Adamson

Shane enjoys date nights with his wife, outings with his family, and relaxing with a good book or movie. Shane volunteers within his church and community. Shane's personal interests are golfing, photography, technology gadgets and the great outdoors. Since moving to Texas, he is learning to BBQ the Texas way.

Shane has worked in both public and private mental health agencies. Shane has 20 years experience with clinical counseling and program development. He is the clinical director of Center for Marriage & Family Counseling. Shane believes that "Family Life" can be the "Center of a Happy Life." Shane gets a front row seat to the many complex relationship problems and mental health challenges that individuals, marriages and families face. Shane believes investing in developing a healthy marriage will bring immense joy and happiness to life. Shane also believes struggle and suffering is a natural part of the human experience. Shane dedicated significant time and training beyond his masters degree to develop specialties in treating mental health issues, addiction and marriage counseling. Shane considers counseling his "life call" and feels honored to witness many amazing things happen in therapy sessions. He considers it a sacred journey to walk along side with clients out of pain and into more peace & well being.

Shane Adamson LCSW
Director Center for Marriage & Family Counseling
www.LifeSTARDallas.com
www.shaneadamson.com
shaneadamsonlcsw@gmail.com
214-250-7808

"Marriage is an adventure where we learn how to love
more deeply and unconditionally."
-    Shane Adamson

# Chapter 4 – The Elevator Dream

# Chapter 4

# The Elevator Dream
By Joe Velazquez

**Washington, D.C.**
There we were, sitting in the office of a U.S. Congressman in Washington, D.C. while attending a conference with the National Association of Hispanic Real Estate Professionals. The small window behind the desk chair offered a sneak view of the Capitol. The sense in the room was official with pictures and other memorials on walls and tabletops that recorded iconic moments. My colleagues and I anxiously awaited the arrival of the Representative. Soon, we were engaged in full conversation, and to my stunning surprise, the dignitary began to inquire about our personal position on issues such as immigration reform. It was a surreal moment as I sat across from this very important person and began to describe my personal story – a first generation immigrant whose father embraced the dream and vision of bringing his family to this great country called America, the Land of Opportunity.

Who would have known that the boy who grew up in the streets of Mexico in a border town from a meek family, learning English as a second language, would one day be walking the Halls of Congress. More so, visiting lawmakers as an advocate for Hispanic Homeownership as well as achieve a career in banking to become a Senior Vice-President for a global financial institution.

## Where it All Began

I will never forget this address: 836 Altamirano Norte, Ciudad Juarez Chihuahua, the place that holds some of the most vibrant memories of my childhood, where I grew up. We were a common Mexican family living in a border town. The neighborhood was alive with pedestrians and family-owned stores like the panaderia (a bakery) in the corner with a wood burning oven. The neighbors were like family. During the summer, parents would gather under a tree and chat while listening to music as my friends and I played soccer in the street. This would go on for hours, night after night. We didn't know what we didn't have, we were rich simply by the nature of our being and cultural synergy – we were a family.

My father, who passed in 1994, is one of the hardest working individuals I have ever known. I watched him go to work early mornings, come home midday, then go back for the evening shift while my mother cared tirelessly for me and my three sisters. For as long as I can remember, he worked as a staff waiter for a prestigious private club known as The El Paso Club. It was located and occupied on the entire 18th floor of the El Paso National Bank Building on Main Street in downtown El Paso, Texas. With a local passport that authorized him to work in the U.S. while living in Mexico, he would commute across the U.S. border for better pay, enabling him to provide the best he could for his family. His work ethic consisted of arriving to work one hour early and being the last one to leave.

My dad didn't know a stranger. I can still visualize walking down the street with him; it was a parade of greetings and salutations, "Hola Don Pepe!" I heard many times as we strolled through downtown or our neighborhood. He modeled the meaning of respecting others regardless of their title or social standing. I witnessed as he would greet a janitor or a homeless person in the same way he would treat a person of stature. He always had change and small bills in his pocket ready to give a hand out to the street bums, which knew him as well for his genuine kindness and generosity.

He was also well acquainted with members of the club who were politicians, attorneys, doctors, successful entrepreneurs, and business professionals. Even in his humble position with a third-grade education, he had a significant network of influential leaders who regarded and spoke highly of him.

**Lydia Patterson Institute**
I went to school in Mexico through the 6th grade. The summer after completing grade school appeared to be the typical school break. However, little did I know a whole new world was about to be revealed before my very eyes; I was

enrolled to start 7th grade in a private school on United States soil. Lydia Patterson Institute was located just south of downtown El Paso. This wasn't the usual path of education for low or moderate income families, especially for students from Mexico, due to the cost of tuition. Nonetheless, both of my parents were compelled and determined to provide for us the opportunity to learn English and have a solid learning foundation. Thanks to the hard work of my father earning a waiter's wage and my mother selling Stanley Home products as an independent distributor, they managed to enroll me and my sisters in this private school. We literally walked to school to another country from Ciudad Juarez to El Paso, and would pass through U.S. Customs to and from school – it was an excursion! I never knew or questioned why we had to work in the school cafeteria during our lunch hour. Now I realize we were working to pay a portion of the tuition. It was during that time I began learning to speak English. I remain forever grateful to those teachers who endured a labor of love to teach and inspire a group of children to press forward, despite adversities, to learn the most widely spoken language in the world. It was a priceless experience and the beginning of a whole new life.

## The ride to the 18th Floor

Sometimes, after school when the El Paso Club was closed in the afternoon, my dad would bring us there as he finished his work for the day. I was always mesmerized as we walked up to the bank tower, a stunning white building standing tall in the middle of downtown. I would glare at the first floor, then with my eyes I would follow its perimeter all the way to the top with my head stretched back as far as I could; it looked as if it kissed the sky. The glass doors at the main entrance would slide open as you stepped on a floor mat, it was magical! The lobby resembled a ballroom with marble floors and a running fountain that stretched from one side of the entrance to the other. Next to the tall glass windows, the sound of running water filled the air creating a soothing atmosphere. Then, we would walk down the hall to a set of huge elevators with brass trimming and numbers on top that lit up to display the location of the cart. The doors would open and there it was: the ride that would transport us to the 18th floor, The El Paso Club.

As soon as I turned 16 years of age I began to work alongside my dad. Most of my high school years and summers I worked as a bus boy. I had the afternoon shift during the week, 4-10pm, 2-11pm on Saturdays, and off Sundays and Mondays. It didn't leave much time for extracurricular activities or time to be with friends. So I would find ways to socialize, which many times meant I would be up late at night. The job required me to maintain certain upkeep in personal grooming and wear a formal classic waiter uniform. It was quite the sight: it consisted of black slacks, crisp ironed white shirt, black bow tie, and the authentic bright orange waste-line waiter's jacket. Oh, and how could I forget the white napkin that hung over my forearm. As you can see, it was the ideal apparel for a teenager! As I rode the elevator every day wearing that uniform, I would ride next to young men and women that worked in the bank, and I would dream about having a job like that one day; where I would wear a suit and tie and be in a business environment. I didn't know it then, but as I reflect on those times, I realize the lessons I learned have been invaluable. My dad was a leader in his own way, he modeled humbleness yet he had a remarkably strong work ethic. He taught me to work with corazón (heart and passion) and to carry out the most insignificant task with superb excellence.

## The Ballroom
My job entailed preparing and setting up the room for elaborate and formal events. As with all endeavors, you must be committed to the process and allow the proper timeline for the vision to blossom and eventually flourish. My work would start with a large ballroom that looked more like an attic with scattered objects such as tables, chairs, and other restaurant paraphernalia. The first step involved creating the layout and location for the number of tables necessary to accommodate the appropriate number of guests. Then, the movement began. Tables were strategically placed throughout the room with accurate distance from one another allowing just enough space for people to mingle during the evening. Once tables and chairs were in place, we began to dress the room. A starched white tablecloth would cover the imperfections of raw round tables followed by a striking centerpiece. Before the silverware was put in place, it was inspected for water marks, many times it required being hand polished to a sparkling shine. Each utensil had to be positioned in the right spot with a specific measurement from the edge of the table, from other pieces, plates, and glasses. Once each piece was laid out, the plates followed. Then, three sets of crystal glasses (one for water,

white wine, and red wine) lit up the table for the final touch. It was an art that required attention to detail, a tremendous amount of patience, precision, and a personal touch of heart and passion. Once the room was completed, the lighting was adjusted and candles would be lit. The room's ambiance was transformed into a glamorous royal atmosphere.

Dreams and visions begin the same way. Allow me to use the analogy of the ballroom to assess the progression of a thought or idea. When a vision surges through your mind, it usually comes with many theories on how you could make it a reality, thus resembling the cluttered ballroom with a number of scattered objects. Those objects are needed to dress the ballroom, yet it will be necessary to organize and select only the essential items required for the job. The same goes for the number of ideas that will flood your mind as you begin to give more thought and energy to your dreams. Think about how utensils had to be inspected before being placed on the table; in the same way, each idea should be examined to ensure it complements the big picture. Focus, patience, along with the most important ingredients, heart and passion, will be absolutely necessary to cross the finish line. Eventually, the dream, which starts in a cluttered space, takes the form of a beautifully panoramic view and provides a memorable and inspiring experience for many.

## You Have Permission to Dream

Every one of us has dream robbers. They come in countless forms, shapes, and sizes. Some are easy to spot and manage, yet some may require the help of others to conquer. Look to identify those things that keep you from allowing your mind to flow in the ability of creativity. For example, the act of assuming could be an offender in this area, which is accepting or believing that certain things will happen without any given action, thus creating a false expectation that our dreams and visions will simply unfold and become a reality without our effort. Another dream robber could be the fear of making or repeating mistakes. I'm here to tell you nothing could be further from the truth. Mistakes are life's guardrails that keep you from completely going over the edge, and with time and a sprinkle of wisdom, they turn into life lessons that mold and shape the best of you. One of the greatest values of failing forward is the capacity to learn from those bloopers, then leverage the experience to mature and impart value in someone else's life. Make an inventory of what your dream robbers might be. Becoming aware of those nagging matters will empower you to see right through them and provide you with the opportunity to address them in a way that becomes favorable to your success. I'm an advocate for personal development, and one effective way to embark on that journey is to find a coach or mentor. It will expand your perspective and will challenge the way you think about yourself and your surroundings. Discover techniques and learning styles that work for you. Become intentionally aware of your aspirations and start dreaming!

**Act on it!**

A dream is fueled by an instinct desire with the ultimate goal to birth an idea or reach a certain goal. I think about my parents and how they fixed their minds on one day calling America our home. They imagined how it would open a pathway to endless possibilities for me and my sisters. To accomplish this epic mission they had to be intentional. My father had to take the initiative to learn about the process, inquire about the prerequisites, and most importantly, submit the application. I challenge you to be proactive about taking the first step towards your God-given desires. Awaken the giant within you, shake off the dream webs, and embark on a deep thinking session about what you need to begin that journey.

"What got you here won't get you there."- Marshall Goldsmith.

Making a choice on how we utilize time is up to each one of us individually. We are all given 24 hours each day; it's up to us how we apply each one of them. Start by blocking time on your calendar and make an appointment for your personal development either daily or weekly. Ask yourself the question, "What are you willing to give up?" For many people, watching a favorite TV show might have to take second or third place, or be completely off the list. In other cases, it might require someone to reassign time being spent in a hobby or interest that draws your attention. You must be willing to trade time, and as you begin negotiating with yourself, visualize what the end result will look like. Yes, the masterpiece you will eventually create.

## Who do you know?
Never underestimate the power and synergy that exists in the realm of the people you know, including acquaintances or friends you have made throughout the years. There lies a tremendous amount of resources waiting to be tapped. Scan your memory bank and look to remember individuals that

have commonality in the area of your dream. Perhaps it's a former colleague, friend, someone you grew up with, or an association you are a member of. This is a pool of potential connectors. Many of them already operate as agents of hope. I have been fortunate in many occasions where, by reaching out to a friend or someone I know and asking for a simple favor, it made all the difference in getting things done or closing the deal. Practice leveraging the power of who you know.

"Any time you see a turtle up on top of a fence post, you know he had some help."- Alex Haley.

## Know your strengths

As I began my career as a mail clerk at El Paso National Bank, I recognized connecting with people and creating relationships came naturally to me. Every day as I walked my route throughout the floors of the bank building, I got to see and meet firsthand the staff in every department. It didn't feel like a job. I was in my element, my strength zone – connecting with people. I began to exercise that gift and put it to practice by initiating small talk with people throughout the route and asking questions about their role and department. From those conversations and my curiosity, I learned that Trust Banking was intriguing to me. One day as I delivered the mail to that department, I told the manager I would be highly interested in working for him and asked to consider me next time he had an opportunity. To my surprise, a few months later an opening came up in the Trust Library and guess who got the job – yours truly! Here is the point: You must become fully aware of your best skills, acknowledge and polish them. Aligning those attributes with your dreams and visions, combined with action, your level of confidence will skyrocket resulting in promotion and success. Take account of your individual qualities and capacities. This is a collage of things you're passionate about, activities you enjoy, what moves you or breaks your heart, the kind of music you prefer, what type of environment makes you flourish in creativity and performance, so on and so forth. By bringing these factors to a high-level of consciousness and taking action, the impact you will have in every area of your life will magnify.

"The privilege of a lifetime is to become who you truly are." – C.G. Jung

| Strengths | | Awareness (I know who I am) | | | | Confidence |
|---|---|---|---|---|---|---|
| God-Given Talents | + | Development of Strengths | + | ACTION | = | Promotion |
| Natural Attributes | | Focus | | | | Success |

"You don't have to be great to start, but you have to start to become great." -Joe Sabah

If there is one message I have especially for young professionals that also applies to everyone, it is to begin now. Don't put your dreams on the shelf thinking you'll reach for them once you're ready. There are great benefits in planning and measuring risk; the problem is when we analyze until we're paralyzed. For some people, starting the journey may be doing something as simple as taking a course to increase their level of expertise or knowledge. Others have the stomach to plunge right in and never look back. Regardless of what your pace may be, embark on fulfilling your desired livelihood today. You will look back one day and be glad you did.

I discovered career aspirations and dreamed of a successful future while riding an elevator, in a building in downtown El Paso, on my way to a job as a waiter. By the grace of God and the support of numerous people, coaches, mentors, managers, friends, and even strangers throughout my entire life, today I have an accomplished career in banking that extends to three decades. Activating that dream and vision gave life to many branches of opportunities and discovery of talents I developed throughout the years. The highlight of my tenure in Corporate America has been the time I devoted as an advocate to advance homeownership for low-moderate income and multicultural families. This cooperative effort facilitated an opportunity for many families to become homeowners.

As I reflect back to that day in Washington D.C. as my colleagues and I anxiously waited to meet with a member of the U.S. House of Representatives, I am extremely grateful for the opportunities this great country has bestowed upon me and my family. The most exciting part of it all is: the best is yet to come...

- Joe Velazquez

## About the Author – Joe Velazquez

Jose (Joe) Velazquez is a first-generation immigrant who learned English as a second language at a young age. He became a U.S. Resident at the age of 13, thanks to the vision and tenacity of his parents. He grew up in El Paso Texas; his first job in banking was as a Mail Clerk at El Paso National Bank in 1984. He made Dallas Fort Worth his home in 1991. Joe is a husband, married to Ruby for 23 years, and a father to three amazing young men.

His career in banking extends over three decades with collective experience in Mortgage Banking, Multicultural Markets, Community Affairs, Community Development, Real Estate Marketing, and Trust Banking. Throughout his career he has been a homeownership advocate especially for low-moderate income and multicultural communities.

He is a former President of the Dallas Hispanic Bankers Association, and the North Texas Chapter of the National Association of Hispanic Real Estate Professionals. He was appointed to Vice-Chair Commissioner of the Dallas Housing Authority by the Mayor of the City of Dallas, and served as a Board Director in numerous civic organizations.

He is a co-author and Certified Speaker by the John Maxwell Team. His mission is to live a legacy of generosity, prosperity, and adding value to others. He believes in the power of giving back, the power to dream and to prosper in every area of our lives. He is passionate about making a positive impact in people's life personally and professionally.

- Joe Velazquez

817-988-3992
FB: @joevelazquezspeaker
LinkedIn: www.linkedin.com/in/joe-velazquez-5a154043
Email: Joe.velazquez@sbcglobal.net

Chapter 4 – The Elevator Dream

"Awaken the giant within you, shake off the dream webs, and embark on a deep-thinking session about what you need to begin that journey."
-    Joe Velazquez

# Chapter 4 – The Elevator Dream

# Chapter 5

# Why You Should Love Lemons
By Shanna Dorion

**No Pressure, No Lemonade**

At work, at home, with relationships, and with life in general, EVERYTHING HAPPENS ON PURPOSE! Everything has a purpose – even lemons. The good, the bad, the ugly, the sour and the sweet, and the highs and the lows; EVERYTHING works together! All things work together for good to them that believe (Romans 8:28). There are no coincidences. There's nothing we can't bear. Lemons are just life's little lessons waiting to teach us something unforgettable and great. Like turning lemons into lemonade, it's the sour being prepped for the sweet. It took me so long to figure this out, but I get it. FINALLY!! I get it! Better late than never, right?

Here's what I've learned in my years of being on this earth: It's not what happens to you that counts, it's how you handle what happens to you that counts. I feel the need to repeat. It's not what happens to you that counts, it's how you handle what happens to you that counts and, how you view it. It's not about the "what," it's about "you." This has everything to do with you. You control your destiny. You control how you react. You control your emotions. You control your thoughts. You control what you do. You, you, you. Point blank! How you view the good, the bad, and the ugly, the highs and the lows, and the sour and the sweet, is up to you. Do you have a glass half-full mentality or a glass half-empty mentality? Are you a happy person or a sad person? Hmmm…Think about it. This makes all the difference in the world. You have the power to change your life.

Allow me to take a little stroll down memory lane. I remember telling myself, on many occasions, "Here's the hand you've been dealt, Shanna. It is out of your control." It was so easy to fall off and focus on the negatives, and it was so hard to find the positives.

For example, when things didn't go my way, I falsely told myself: unanswered prayers – they don't work! "No!" I shouted to my mother, "Everything will not be OK, so stop saying that it will. How long do I have to wait? I am tired of waiting. I am tired of believing. Why is it so hard for me to get anything? Why do I have to work 10 times harder than everybody else to get ahead? Nothing will ever change." This was my outlook on life and relationships and my career. I'm shaking my head just thinking about it. Imagine your heart, the thing that gives you life, taking a bite into a big, fat, juicy lemon. Over and over again, I was biting into lemons, lemons, lemons, and it made me sick. Literally.

Not married, no children, and not where I felt I deserved to be professionally. Check this out: I read an article once, which stated *one out of four women won't get married.* "OMG," I thought, "Could this be me? Am I the one? After all, I did

have three best friends. Nooooo," I pleaded, "Please God!"
I felt like a failure. And like a broken record, to sooth my
pain, my dad would often say, "Don't linger on the negatives,
Shanna. Let that go. Don't dwell on it. You're gonna give
yourself a heart attack." But I didn't know how to let it go. I
wasn't ready to let it go. The even crazier thing was, I didn't
want to let it go. Sad, but true. Hands thrown in the air. Big
sigh. Breathe Shanna, breathe. All you have to do is breathe.

I used to complain. I was the victim. Everyone was against
me. I complained to anyone who would listen; coworkers,
the people down the hall at work, family, and friends. And
to think, after a while, people started avoiding me. *What?! The
nerve!* Automatically I believed that other people (the enemy)
had gotten to them, filling their heads with vicious lies about
me. It was the victimization mentality in full effect, and all
along, it was me. I was sabotaging myself. Nobody, but me.
Can you believe that? It was that horrible mindset of mine.
My thought process was killing every area of my life.

Let me rewind a little more. Just so you get a clear picture of
how I grew up. I grew up in a small, but fun and growing
little city in southern Louisiana. In fact, I am proud to tell
you that my city was recently voted the happiest city in the
U.S. How cool is that? Family, friends, party, and prayer is
our way of life. I was raised to be polite, respectful,
hospitable, and lady-like. This is our culture. My parents gave
my brother and me the best, most invaluable gift any parents
can give their children: unconditional love. They sacrificed,
worked super hard, and invested their time and love to keep

our family happy, healthy, and whole. Excellent providers indeed. They were selfless.

Our home, it was big and beautiful. We had large pine trees perfect for a lazy swing on a warm and breezy summer day. I have so many wonderful memories at that house: riding my bike, playing with neighborhood friends, sleepovers, tons of family gatherings, bar-b-ques, walking to the pond, the ducks and duck eggs, the red wagon, and helping mom with garage sales. Only memories of blessings and love and sunshine. Well, in the 80s during the big oilfield bust, the unimaginable happened. My dad was laid off. My parents bared socioeconomic hardships and as a result, we lost our home! They were devastated. I saw their devastation. They were embarrassed and I saw their embarrassment. Not only did this take a huge toll on them, but even as a child, eight years of age with pigtails to be exact, this took a huge toll on me. The only home I'd known was no longer my home.

My mom, the most loyal woman I know, experienced discrimination on her job. She also worked in the oilfield industry. We were the typical southern oilfield family. In her role, she trained and supervised employees, followed orders to the T, and barely ever missed a day of work. Nonetheless, she was belittled, passed over, taken for granted, and her salary was like highway robbery. I remember her complaining, every - single - day. She hated that place. She hated how she was treated. She felt cheated. She was miserable. Yet, she remained loyal to those people. WHY? She took that buffoonery and abuse for almost 30 years and to add insult to injury, she was laid off.

Unfortunately, these experiences made my parents fearful and suspicious about so many things. Things like people, intentions, motives, promises, risks, challenges, opportunities, failure, you name it. In the same breath, they encouraged my brother and me. They made us study. They taught us to save money, especially dad. That was his thing. They taught us to pray and they made us go to church. They taught us the golden rule: "Do unto others as you would have them do unto you." (Matthew 7:12) They made sure we kept good company. Still, in that same breath, being "realistic" was their approach. They knew their "spot" in this world. For them, equal opportunities would be almost impossible living in the south, based on past experiences. After all, the best indicator of future opportunities are past opportunities, right? They were traumatized, and rightfully so.

Although they did their absolute best for us, seeing their suspicion made me fearful, untrusting, defensive, and "victimized." Still, I had a burn in my bones. I wanted to do better; I wanted to do more. No matter how hard things seemed, I refused to give up. I wanted to win in life. Deep down, I wanted to believe for better. I wanted to reach for the stars and look fancy doing it. I'll just sip my lemonade, smile, and continue to dream BIG.

Mom would say to me, "If you believe it, you can achieve it, and if you put your mind to it you can do it." What she said really stuck. As I got older, I knew she regretted instilling that in me. She tried to talk me out of doing many things. She didn't want to see me hurt if I failed. This made me want "it" more. I wanted to show her and my dad that I could do it. I tried so many different things and failed. Tried again and failed again. Then finally, finally, I'd get a win! With no intention of my own, I developed a spirit of tenacity. I just wanted what I wanted so badly. I tried hard. I figured if I didn't quit, eventually, I would win. A painful, uncomfortable recurrence, but for me, a necessary recurrence.

Yes, I was afraid of failure, but I refused to let failure stop me. Perhaps my desire to BE MORE was bigger than my fear of failure and bigger than the discomfort. My mom had instilled in me the "if you believe it, you can achieve it," mentality, so much so that it scared her. I explored big things. I thought, "I'm going to try it. I want it! Why not me?" Part of this desire came from my parents paying close attention to my friends. They only allowed me to socialize with peers who were respectful, goal oriented, and well-spoken. Praise the Lord! I tell you, the company you keep can do either one of two things: they can elevate and encourage you, or they can bring you down and discourage you. Yes, it is that crucial. Luckily for me, I aimed high with selecting my friends. They were so smart. They were ambitious. They pushed me. I aspired to do what they were doing and be just as successful. I aspired to be bigger than my circumstances.

Unbeknownst to what was happening to me at that time was that my core was strengthening. I was being molded and prepared for my destiny. My foundation was being built. The more I matured, the more this was evident. Still hard and still uncomfortable, but still determined to move forward. I remember thinking, "My goodness, something's got to give."

Knowing that the process is necessary, I wondered, "What can I do to make this process of life, the squeeze, which is so uncomfortable, not so uncomfortable and not so painful?" I didn't know the answers until a few years back. Well, actually, I've known the answers all along, I just didn't know it then. Perhaps I didn't believe it. I definitely didn't know how to apply it because the answer is multifaceted and it requires creativity and open-mindedness. Here's the key: the answer to making the process of life, the squeeze, not so uncomfortable is only correct when added together with other components, like pieces of a puzzle or parts of an equation.

**The first part of the equation: Selective Memory!**

It was during this time that I started squeezing lemons, mixing it with a shot of resilience, and later on in life, as I matured, adding a pinch of selective memory. The selective memory part worked awesome for me. I tried my best to forget about past failures, so that it wouldn't stop me from dusting myself off, getting back up, and trying again. I didn't know it yet, but this was the beginning of my process of turning lemons into pitchers of good 'ole fashioned Louisiana Lemonade. I was like a lemon being squeezed tightly under pressure. This lemon is a necessary ingredient. The squeeze is necessary for the juice. It's all necessary! It's all relevant. No pressure, no lemonade. No lemon, no lemonade.

In my search for the answer, I began by asking myself, "What are you going to do about particular situations, circumstances, or issues?" These issues could be barriers keeping me back, like not getting a promotion. To remedy the situation, and to continue to move forward, I grew in my selective memory. I worked hard on only remembering what was helpful and forgetting the rest. I focused on the lesson. In doing so, I kept no record of the losses. I lead myself to believe that I could create my own opportunities by continuing on with energy and enthusiasm. This gave me a second wind. It's almost like I was tricking myself or my mind. "What failure?" Like a child or a spouse or a colleague or a customer who only hears what they want to hear, that's what I did with my memory. I chose what I wanted to remember.

OK, now that I had the selective memory in place, I had to keep the momentum going, stay strong, and stay focused on my dreams. Heck, I'm human. I already know I'll have moments of temptation. Even Jesus was tempted, so who am I to think that I won't be? Clearly, I am not as strong as He is! I already know that I will have moments of weakness, setbacks, discouragement, disappointment, doubt, sadness, anger, and obstacles to face. Since preparation is super important to me, I asked myself more questions. Questions like: What will keep me motivated? What will make the process even smoother? What will make it fun? Is fun even possible? Yep, POSITIVELY so. Well, how can that be accomplished? Through positivity! That's it.

**This is another part of the equation: Positivity!**
Positivity begets positivity. Only speaking kindly of myself and to myself made me feel in control of my life. Having positive thoughts and positive words, allowed me to refocus my energy on what was uplifting. I believed that I would win no matter what. I force-fed this philosophy to myself. Here's what I mean: Winning is a state of mind. So is failure. And moral victories can be found in every situation, right? Right! If I tried and I failed, I told myself, "At least I tried, when most people wouldn't have tried. I am one step closer to my goal." That was a moral victory. If I failed, I did not view it as failure, I viewed it as a valuable lesson learned which would not have been obtained otherwise. A moral victory indeed! If I finished last that meant I didn't quit. Moral victory! If a relationship ended or if I didn't get the job, I believed I was being saved from a bullet. "Phew!" I would say, "Thank you, Jesus, for saving me from what would have been a disaster." If I got caught in traffic, held up by a train, or couldn't manage to put my hands on my keys, I would chuckle and tell myself that I have been kept from an accident. Thank you, Jesus, for saving me. I looked for the positives, NO MATTER WHAT. Everything happens for a reason and in the end, greatness will be the result. I reminded myself this constantly! I force-fed this to myself, constantly, so that I would never forget. Made the lemons pretty easy to gobble down. That mindset is major!

In order to be positive, you have to shake things up big time! Making the shift to a positive mindset is a change, a major one, on the inside and out. For instance, I started distancing myself from negative people. I realized negativity is toxic and negative people are toxic, too. I realized that not everyone would understand my drive, my passion, my dreams, or my enthusiasm. I realized that I couldn't share my heart's desires with everyone because not everyone would be happy for me or my success or my growth. This included acquaintances, friends, and yes, even family. Distancing yourself is a tough thing to do, especially if you're soft-hearted like me, but it is super necessary. After all, misery really does love company. And, if I try to force-feed them my philosophies, they will burst my positive bubble.

A few people even made the "cut" list. If you're draining me, you've got to go. If you're not adding value to my life, you've got to go. If you have a negative outlook, you've got to go. This is what I like to call "weeding season." Pull out the bad weeds. Not just people, but my own thoughts and words and actions had to be weeded. Weeds will eventually take over and destroy a beautiful garden. Weeding season is so necessary. It was necessary for me and it is necessary for you. It must be done often. Yes, it is hard and uncomfortable, but this is the only way to maintain a positive attitude. It takes courage, bravery, and boldness to do this, but I am a happier and healthier person because of it.

Trying to be positive in all situations can be testing, but with time, patience, practice and perseverance, it gets easier, and it becomes a part of you. I've heard it said before that loss can be the best change. I believe that. This is what I call a blessing in disguise. Here's an example: I got laid off from my job. However, getting laid off from my job made me more positive. Weird, huh? But it's true. At that point, I decided this was the perfect opportunity for me to start my own business. I was excited about the future. This was like graduation for me, baby! Yes, I decided to stop complaining about things that were out of my control. I decided to stop listening to my ego and the naysayers because doing so made me bitter. I made the choice to believe that the timing of this layoff was perfect and so was the outlet. I believed that this was exactly what I needed: the push! I made the decision to turn that lemon into some good, sweet, ice-cold lemonade.

During this time, colleagues were falling sick. A couple colleagues were even taken out of the office on stretchers due to anxiety and being overcome by fear. However, throughout this unfortunate and untimely situation, I managed to bounce around in a little positive bubble. Some thought I would fail in my new business endeavor. Some tried to talk me out of it. Some thought it was a dumb thing to do. Some thought I was crazy. However, many came to me for advice because of my positivity. I stayed strong by speaking only positive words, words of encouragement, and words to inspire hope. Through doing this, it made me better, more positive, and even more confident that everything would work out regardless of what happens. Immediately following the layoff, I started my business, and I am happy to say that I have been in business for over two years now.

So, now you've got selective memory and positivity in the equation. What next?

**The final part of the equation is faith.**
Yep, good 'ole fashioned faith. Without faith, positivity and selective memory will not work. They will not stand the test of time. They won't be able to fully endure the squeeze. Faith must be included in the equation. Faith is how you muster up the courage to apply the selective memory and positivity time after time again.

Faith is the foundation. Without faith, the process would be too uncomfortable, too painful, too dreadful, and too long to bear. Without faith, you cannot withstand. Without faith, it is impossible to fathom the fact that everything, and I mean everything, is simply a part of the process, and the process is necessary. Faith builds muscles, knowledge, wisdom, drive, relationships (personal and professional), and opportunities. You must have faith.

All you need is a little faith. Even if it's only the size of a tiny lemon drop, it will build you up, push you, keep you focused, keep you strong, keep you sane, and keep you believing that you can win. You will win, no matter how many times you've failed. Faith is what allows you to run the race with endurance. Faith allows you to focus on the finish line and enjoy the journey. Faith is what helps you see that failure, setbacks, loss, and discouragement are only temporary. Faith is what allows you to dance in the rain. Faith helps you to be more patient. Faith is what allows you to plant your seeds and wait with expectancy for your crops to grow. To have faith is to let go and trust the process. Faith is what carries everything. Faith is like sugar. It is what makes the lemons not so sour.

How does one acquire this thing called faith? I am not completely sure. But, what I can tell you is how I acquired my faith. First of all, it did not come easily, naturally, or automatically. It took me to reach my lowest low to seek change. When I realized my way wasn't working, (the misery, confusion, anger, chaos, sickness) I realized I had to do something different, something major. I was running on empty. My faith was all I had to fall back on.

Since I love music, I began listening to praise and inspiration music. I listened all day long. It brought me so much joy and peace to hear positive words: words of victory and hope and love and encouragement. I would walk around singing and playing those songs in my head throughout the day instead of thoughts of worry, defeat, and fear. The sweet melodies and messages of those songs hit a homerun in my core. It is amazing how what we listen to can affect us tremendously. What we listen to can affect the way we see things, our perspectives, our thoughts, the way we walk, talk, think, and feel. Whether it be for good or for bad, the outcome depends on us. It depends on what we choose to feed our minds. I've learned that if I feed my mind and my heart with faith, love, hope, inspiration, and encouragement, my words and behaviors and feelings will reflect that. "For out of the overflow of his heart, his mouth speaks." (Luke 6:45)

I committed to being an active member of my church and our church choir. Not only did I buy a Bible, I started reading it. Yes, I started reading it! I prayed. I attended Bible study. I began to attend church religiously and read the Bible willingly in my quest to find true peace and joy. I sought for these things diligently. I watched tons of inspirational videos and sermons. I subscribed to faith-based social media networks.

In addition, I made a healthy habit of having gratitude and appreciating everything I have. I practice gratitude the minute I open my eyes. When I hop out of bed in the morning, I immediately turn on praise and inspiration music. I put positive scriptures everywhere, on mirrors, too. Doing these things fill me up, make me smile, and make me dance early in the morning, even while brushing my teeth. I can't contain it. That's faith, baby! Wholesome, pure, faith. No matter the situation, you are able to find peace. You are able to smile, laugh lavishly, and live life on purpose.

We must remember that we will have ups and downs, rain and sunshine. After all, isn't the rain necessary for flowers to grow and strong oaks to take root? This is normal; this is the beauty of life! Besides, how boring would life be if everything were easy? All we have to do is get through the sour with a little grace and finesse and strength.

## Selective Memory + Positivity + Faith

Now, I cannot promise that this formula will work for you, nor do I claim for it to work immediately or magically or be the ultimate cure-all. However, I definitely can guarantee that it will lighten your load tremendously, bring you joy, and increase your quality of life if you practice it diligently.

All of these components are necessary to excel in life, sanely and joyfully, with less discomfort.

Applying the selective memory will allow us to forget the bad things and only focus on what's helpful so that we can move forward with energy and enthusiasm. Applying the positivity piece will allow us to drive out the negatives and find the positives in every situation. Positivity begets positivity! This creates a happy zone during the journey. The final piece, the anchor of selective memory and positivity is Faith! You need this final piece; without it, all you have is a bunch of lemons. Without faith, Life will leave you with a sour taste in your mouth. Faith must be applied daily. No Faith = No Lemonade.

If we approach the process of life, the squeeze, with the right attitude, finding the positives and letting go of the rest, applying a little faith and some selective memory, it will make this thing called life so much smoother and sweet. That is quality. That is what life is all about.

If you love the sweet taste of lemonade, you gotta love the lemons too. Nobody said life would be easy, but isn't life so much more enjoyable sipping on a hard-squeezed glass of cold lemonade than sucking on a peel?

- Shanna Dorion

*I failed, I feared, I fought*
*I fought, I feared, I failed*
*I cried, I didn't understand*
*I could not see*
*Everything that was happening,*
*Was growing me.*

## Chapter 5 – Why You Should Love Lemons

*A heart of hope, A heart to help, A heart of love*
*Yet still, It was hard*
*to rise above.*

*Why me? I asked myself*
*So many obstacles*
*So plain to see*
*And the naysayers – they're plenty*

*But I try so hard...*
*Work, Worry, Complain, Maintain*
*Ms. People Pleaser*
*Could be my name*
*Am I the one to blame?*

*What could it be?*
*Something's gotta give*
*I gotta stay the course*
*I want to live!*

*Live Big, Live Freely, Live Happily, Live Strong*
*Ain't nothing wrong with that*
*I'm human, you see*
*All of these experiences were necessary for me*
*to have a foundation, and flexibility as strong as a palm tree*
*NO LEMONS NO LEMONADE*
*I wouldn't change a thing!*
*I feel the breeze*
*I taste the sweet*
*Thank God for Changing Me!*

## About the Author – Shanna Dorion

Shanna M. Dorion is the epitome of passion and excitement. Her flair as a trainer, speaker, and success coach is refreshing, energizing, and contagious. Wrapped in a colorful bundle of real world experiences, Shanna shares her best practices, lessons learned, and tried and true methods of success to help individuals and businesses shine bright.

Shanna is a positivity promoter, confidence creator and professionalism expert. Her focus is on leadership, client services, communication, and business etiquette. She is known for her ability to connect with her clients and audiences. Shanna's message is engaging and informative with a sprinkle of humor and a pinch of fun.

Shanna is certified and endorsed by the Ziglar Corporation and the American School of Protocol. She brings 16 years of retail banking, sales, service and training experience. She is the proud owner and founder of Biz Knocks, a professional development and character education company. Shanna is in the business of people polishing. She aims to infuse her clients with the tips and tools that they need to be their absolute best.

No matter your industry or title, if communicating with others is a part of your role, you are encouraged to contact Shanna. Businesses, if your goal is to increase performance, moral, and client satisfaction, you are encouraged contact Shanna. She is excited to serve.

When business knocks, be ready!

Contact

Shanna Dorion
Training and Development Specialist
Biz Knocks
office: (337) 534-4424
email: shanna@bizknocks
website: www.Bizknocks.com
Facebook, Twitter, LinkedIn

"All you need is a little faith. Even if it's only the size of a tiny lemon drop, it will build you up, push you, keep you focused, keep you strong, keep you sane, and keep you believing that you can win."
-    Shanna Dorion

# Chapter 5 – Why You Should Love Lemons

# Chapter **6**

# From Zero to Abundance
By Olusola Andrew Omole

## THE JOURNEY

As our plane took off from Manchester, UK to Dallas Texas, there was an excitement welling up in me. Although flying is not one of my best experiences as I resent the security hoops I needed to jump through at the airport to get seated on the plane. This was my first trip to the US and I had my lovely wife with me. We lead very busy lives and with two young children to look after, we don't often get the luxury of being by ourselves, whether to rest or catch some fun. This promises to be a great time for her as she will be able take the much-deserved rest she so craved. She had worked so hard few months back to ensure our business achieved a good rating from government regulators.

For me, there was more to my excitement. It wasn't about catching some fun or taking a rest, as I have never been one crazy about holidays. I am always working. Even when we decide to take time out, I still find myself secretly working, to my wife's wrath. I guess this has to do with the foundation

83

I had growing up. My dad was very hardworking. He used to have acres of a plantation farm where he spent most of his weekends, so watching TV or just lying on the couch for him, is indicative of not having enough to do. He would call out and say, 'Son, you have to be productive.' These were words I heard almost daily and I guess they still ring in my ears today.

The prospect of becoming a Legacy Certified Trainer was icing on my cake. I felt that I could at least be a part of something significant. Something that would outlast me. Something that generations after me will live to remember me for. It would add some credibility to my name and be adopted in to one of the world's best families. A family that values individuals and upholds integrity with all sense of responsibility. It would be a boost to my informal training, coaching, and mentoring ministry, which I developed over the years working with a fairly large youth group within our local church. I was looking forward to the training, as I believed it would enable me to give back more to my world.

My excitement increased as I landed in the DFW Airport. It was a bright sunny day; a great deviation from the cold weather of Manchester. I had a sense something was about to change for me. I couldn't place my finger on it, but it was so strong. We picked up a nice luxury car at the airport and rolled in style to our hotel. I had a night to rest before the start of my certification training.

Then it all began to unfold! Little did I know that from the certification class, something new would be birthed in me: a desire stronger than I've ever felt before. Something that started growing from that time and it is still growing now. A desire to see other people become significant. A desire to see others become who God has ordained them to be in grand style. A desire to see humanity exchange mediocrity and obscurity for greatness and light. This desire was so strong as I saw a message flash through my eyes whilst I sat in training on the first day. As I entered the HQ where my training would take place, I began to see different messages on the wall that caught my eye, but none did so much to me than the one that read – **'You can have everything in life you want if you will just help enough other people get what they want.'**

I had seen this quote before, but on this day something turned loose in me. The pathway to my success is to help other people succeed. The more people I could help to succeed, the more successful I would become. It was a no-brainer! Where was I all these years? Then, my certification meeting was over. God brought me all the way across the Atlantic to show me this message and boy did I get it. This, for me, is like when a scripture I have read over and over just comes alive in a service. I went to the certification for personal development, possibly to help our ever-growing number of staff, parents, and the youths in our local church who come to me for help and advice. I felt the certification would help me to help them more. **Little did I know this would change my life forever.**

## Chapter 6 – From Zero to Abundance

You see, my life's journey started in a very well planned way by my creator. I am not going to start by saying that I was poor and tell all those 'from rags to riches' stories that people put together to stir up your emotions. I believe that every lesson in the journey called 'life' has a divine implication.

Many years ago, I was born in Newcastle Upon Tyne when my father was studying for his doctorate degree. After finishing, he decided to moved back home to Africa as he secured a great job in a renowned Research Institute. I did not have a say in the matter, so I was taken back to my fatherland along with my elder brother and there began my journey.

Growing up was great. We had everything provided. My dad was doing well as a Research Scientist and we lived in a private area of the institute surrounded by a beautiful, well-landscaped green belt area. I would wake up to the sound of birds singing and monkeys chattering and gibbering. You could see them joyously jumping from one tree to another. Thinking about it now, it was such a great view. I attended a private school and one of the best secondary schools at the time in the town where we lived. A staff bus would pick us up and drop us back home. Life was great growing up. Although dad was always away on station assignment, my mum was always there. She instilled discipline and the fear of God in our hearts.

Spare the rod and spoil the child was not a relevant proverb in our home. The rod was always available. If you would err, you would pay for it dearly. If you were good, you were duly rewarded. Church was also a mandatory part of my growing up. It was not optional. To be honest, I never liked church whether going with my dad or mum. The only time I enjoyed it was when I was having ice-cream and visiting my dad's friend or cousins when the service was over. It was just not my thing at the time. I did not understand why we had to be there and why we were obligated to do all we were made to do. Everything at that time seemed to be against my will. You were made to pray, memorise the scriptures, and recite them in the presence of all in Sunday school. My mum was obsessed with Jesus and she still is. I was obliged to be in church every Sunday and Tuesday. However, I can boldly say that the greatest activity of my growing up that still has an impact on my life to date is the relationship that I grudgingly built with that God whose presence I did not enjoy at the time. My relationship with Him directs, guides, encourages, motivates, and spurs me on every day.

In 2002, I decided to return to the UK, and this was where it began to unfold. How it all came to be was just surreal. At this point, my father had retired from his research and project work and it was not in my agenda to rely on him or anyone for my upkeep. I had met the Lord during my 2nd year of university and I was learning to trust Him for all my needs. After I graduated, I started my compulsory national service and was earning only N7,500 naira per month (approximately $23.00).

On a sunny Sunday afternoon, I was with a group of youths from the church we attended in Lagos. We were working to complete the first floor of the church building, when I saw a scene flash across my eyes. I saw myself driving on the motorway in a place signposted 'London.' I whispered to my fiancée (now my wife) what I had seen. She smiled and looked at me in amazement because what I just said had no bearing on what was happening at the time and I had no capacity to accomplish what I just told her. You can't blame her for her reaction. Traveling abroad at that point was a big deal. It was like hitting a jackpot. It was an assumption that money is picked on the streets abroad. This was around March 2002. At that point, I did not have any understanding of the process; I had never bothered to ask. It had never crossed my mind that I may travel abroad for any reason. My mindset has always been that wherever I find myself, the Lord will prosper me there. I never held a passport. I travelled on my mum's passport as a baby, so I did not have one of my own. The thought of owning one had never crossed my mind. What for? I had only a birth certificate, which had always been in a little file carried around by my mum as we moved from place to place. I did not have much at that time, but I was reasonably contented.

Moreover, at that point, I did not have any justifiable savings to undertake the process of getting a passport, or so I thought. In fact, put together my salary and my fiancée's totaled N10000 naira (approximately $32.00). My flight ticket would cost me between N200,000 - N250,000 Naira (approximately $634 - $790) excluding all other passport processing expenses. I was not in a position to even afford a quarter of it, not to mention the full price, but as you may or may not know, 'every vision is for an appointed time' Habakkuk 2:3. After I saw and spoke about it, something in me started driving me towards its accomplishment.

When I received my salary, I had a well-planned out and consistent spending pattern. My tithe and offering went out first. I started tithing as a young Christian in the university after I 'saw' it myself from the scripture. I wrote some time ago, after a study, that **'What you are taught, you may likely forget, but your discoveries stay with you for life.'** Even when one of my dad's friends tried to dissuade me, it was too late! I had 'seen' it and I was not letting it go. Most of the things I learnt in the faith were things I mostly discovered by myself. Tithing & offering was one of them and it is still part and parcel of me today. After my tithe, offering, and any kingdom investment, I gave N500 Naira ($2) to a widow in our local assembly monthly after her husband died. I then set aside another N1000 Naira ($4) for monthly shopping, N500 Naira ($2) for books/CDs from my mentor and the rest went into a savings account. It was a monthly routine and I felt so privileged and blessed that I could save some money out of little.

I can't hand-on-heart explain to you how I survived, but I did. The only thing I was sure of was that I learnt how to manage little resources that God gave me with contentment. I was prudent. Almost all He gave to me at that time went back to Him, but I was very sure He would sustain me.

Little did I know that God was training me and my wife-to-be for such periods as we are in now. We are now truly blessed. Finance is never a topic of discussion, rather it is more of being in God's will more than anything.

During our courtship, I did not have all the good times that people around me who were in relationships were having. They used to go out eating on weekends and do all sorts of fun activities, but we were either in evangelism, prayer meetings, or school of ministry. It is hard for youths to believe me when I speak about it now but that is the truth and we are the best for it. I can't remember us going out to eat or to the cinema, etc. On the contrary, we engaged in sharing God's great love with people everywhere. It is one activity I recommend to everyone for testing the personality tendencies of your wife or husband to be. This is because in evangelism it is difficult to predict the reception you are going to get. You can be speaking to a receptive person now and the next minute to an irritable person. We were able to laugh off our disappointment and move on to the next potential disciples. We were also able to convince some and celebrate the victory together. I recommend this for young people in courtship rather than eating out, which is mostly superficial. We also prayed together for people and their needs and were never the centre of attention. Anyway, all worked out and my trip to the UK was set. It took me approximately three weeks from submission of my documents to the collection of my British passport in Lagos. No begging, no scheming, just trusting. Miraculously, my plane ticket was bought for me and a small stipend put together for me was handed over by my dad. He was so reluctant to let me go. Since leaving the UK in the 70s, he has not been back. I don't think he particularly enjoyed the weather and the loneliness he faced in those days.

## From Zero to Abundance

I flew into London aboard a Lufthansa airline in November 2002. I was armed only with the promises God gave to me when I asked him if this trip met with His will for my life. I knew only two people in the UK. I had been advised by my father that his childhood friend who lived in Manchester would be on hand to meet me, but he was unavailable on the day that I landed. Fortunately, one of my good friends in Lagos was on hand to meet me. Even though my arrangements were not well solidified, I knew God promised me that His angels would go before me.

I converted the money that I had with me to pounds and it came to a total of £970. The amount at that time was the largest single currency I have ever handled in my life on a personal level. I wanted to ensure that I made very good use of it. I couldn't afford to call home for money, as that was all they could pull together for me. My friend took me to his flat where I stayed the night. I rang my dad's friend, but he was unavailable. I tried his office and was advised that he was traveling and would be back the next day. About midday, he rang and advised me that he was in Manchester and said that I should take a coach and come there. It was a big relief. I arrived in Manchester late, but safely. It was a Tuesday and I was headed to church in the evening for my first UK service.

The next month after my arrival, I had started applying for jobs and was also praying that the Lord would show me what I needed to do in this land. He had given me a series of promises whilst I prepared to come, but I knew that I had never walked this road before, and only Him could help me. I was trained by my father never to rely on any man. Many times, I saw him refuse to go to other people for help and he would encourage us to be the same. I had written many applications and was told to see a very popular African man who had an agency and he would help people with Support Work. I did, but I knew that was not the plan. Something inside me just said so. He sent me to only one job and that was the last time I worked there. I had no bank account and just applied for my National Insurance (NI) number. It was as I waited that something happened that I believe changed my life forever!

Trusting the Lord has been a key element of my life. I have never been exposed to any other source of help. All we were exposed to was His help. I was in the house one afternoon watching TV, when I heard the voice of the Lord. It was as if a man was talking to me. He said **'GIVE ALL THE MONEY YOU ARE DEPENDING ON AWAY AND LET ME START YOU FROM ZERO. THIS WILL CONFIRM TO YOU THAT I AM THE ONE THAT PROSPERED YOU IN THIS LAND WHEN YOUR DUE TIME COMES.'** This was a real shock to me. How would I get by? Who would cater for me? What if I was thrown out of this house by my host? How would I pay my way? *However, I had trained myself to distinguish the voice of the Lord from the noise in my head.* I quickly started making the plans and started my distribution list. I sent part of it to many charitable organizations that I knew at the time and gave some to the church. Also, I sent some back to my parents who I knew at that time needed the money, some to my fiancée and some to those in my local church. I am sure that they felt I was already doing well. London streets must be laid with gold. However, I was following the lead of the One who sent me to the UK.

After I had given the money away, I had only £97 left. I had gone to the bank and a customer service advisor informed me that I needed to have some money put aside in the bank to be able to open my account. So, I opened the account with the £97. It was all I had in a strange land, but I had all the resources of heaven behind me. A couple of weeks later my hosts travelled to Africa and I was home alone. That was when my first job came calling.

I was flipping through the pages of one of Manchester's free local newspapers on a Thursday when I saw this advertisement for a Retail Assistant position. I had never been in retail, but I had done a lot of selling of my dad's farm produce whilst I was back home. We packaged cassava flour in those days and sold them to people in a shop that my mum operated on our street back home. We also had a few other items in her shop from one of her sisters who lived with us at the time. Growing up, I sold roasted meat popularly known as 'Suya' and helped with her commercial blender.

# Chapter 6 – From Zero to Abundance

As far as I was concerned, retail for me was the art of buying and producing cheap and selling at a higher price.

I sensed something good would happen with this job, so I applied. I was immediately called for an interview and to my surprise, I was offered a job to start in two days. That was the start of my employment in the UK. My hourly rate was £3.50 at a shop attached to a fuel station on a Road Close to my host house. It was a shift based job and I enjoyed it. My manager was an elderly lady, who was very kind to me and gave me the opportunity to learn quickly. I knew it was a stepping stone for me, but I had to learn fast. It wasn't easy at the start, as the accents would throw me off balance and some of the customers were in a hurry going to work, especially on the morning shift. However, it was my best training ground. I had a mixture of people coming through the door: the rich, the less privileged, the old, and the young. It was a combination of emotions from many of them, but I could handle them all. Before long, I was established and was doing different shift patterns. I was now a trusted and reliable hand. I never called in sick, as I was wired to work hard. I was growing in confidence and influence. My best shift pattern, however, was the night shift. It was my opportunity to talk to God in the quiet of the night. I would pray as I waited for customers who were now far and few between. I would sing as I stacked the shop with goods. Most people were in bed; however, we would get the odd drug dealers, some night crawlers, and prostitutes who worked the nights.

I learnt early in my relationship with God that He would not promote me, no matter how hard I prayed, until I passed His test in the area that I require a breakthrough. My first real test soon came. God had promised me before I left Africa that I would be a blessing to my generation and I enlisted in God's 'Millionaire Club' by faith. I knew God's Millionaires are masters of money. I understood that they are only custodians of God's resources, I knew that He could ask for it at any time. In contrast, I knew that self- proclaimed millionaires are ruled by the love of money and find it hard to let go.

## THE TEST RUN

I was working this blessed evening in the store, I had three young guys walk in. I was sure I had not seen any of them before, but I guess they had kept a watch over me for some time. This was a life experience I couldn't forget in a hurry, but it was a confirmation to me that the fear of God had been perfected in my heart. I wrote sometime ago that '**the love of money will lose its grip over your life when the fear of God is perfected in your life'.** I requested to know how I could help them and they told me they needed to speak to me about something that would excite me when I hear it. As they had been watching me for some months and knew that I recently joined the store. They had put me in the stereotype of those who are desperate for money and would jump at the opportunity to become rich quickly and easily. I was black, young, and very friendly. I ticked all their boxes. This was the period when credit card fraud was rife. No chip and pin technology at the time. They informed me that all I needed to do for them was to remove the link between the till and the phone line and connect a small appliance for them. Every time I would swipe a card across the till, the details would be downloaded directly into their reader and they can use the details to defraud the innocent customers that I was privileged to server. I was offered a **£1000** every week for this seemingly little task. I turned down the offer nicely and informed them of all that God had told me when I was about to move into this great country, about being wealthy, and that none of what they told me was on the list. They were taken aback. They told me how hard it was to make it in the country and how I would thank them when the money started to roll in. I knew the money would as I took a lot of card payments every hour, but I refused.

An hour later, they came back with this other guy who was dressed in all white and had a big chain around his neck. I figured he was the ringleader. Again, he spoke to me and informed me that this would be the best decision of my life. He upped my weekly 'reward of iniquity' to £2000 a week if I did it but I refused and maintaining my initial stand. He got angry and told me that I would die working in the corner shop with nothing to show. That night I cried again in prayer to God that even though my beginning might be small, I expect my latter end to increase greatly.

## IN A TWINKLE OF AN EYE
We moved from my one bed flat in Bowler Street in 2004 to a three-bedroom council house in Fernhill Drive just as my wife was due to deliver. It was a miracle move as there were

only two of us and you are only guaranteed a two-bed house, but when God sends you to a land, He will ensure that all things work for you in that land.

From this little house, we started our childcare business. I was working with HMRC and my wife was on maternity leave from her job. She didn't want to return to work, so she started looking for something to do. Our pastor's wife, at that time, was looking for someone who could help her keep her son whilst she was at work, so my wife took him as a goodwill gesture to them. It was then the door that would lead to this big business opened. We decided it is best to continue in the line of work she was ding already and so she underwent the childminders training and started working. Little did we know God has a greater agenda. In 2003, in my flat in Bowler, the Lord spoke to me that the liberators of Britain were behind the prison doors and that that he preserved me all this while to lead this army of liberators, and that I should be ready to undertake this great agenda. It was a very clear encounter as I was in prayers and study, and one that I wrote down without ambiguity. I wasn't quite sure what He fully meant, but I was sure there was something great God wanted to do. The Bible says we know in parts, so I just had to be sensitive to the timing.

We carried on doing the childcare business with integrity and God continued to increase us. We employed two ladies on our staff team in our terraced house. We were inspected by OFSTED (UK childcare regulators) and were graded 'Outstanding', The Council in the area where we lived started to take notice of our setting. It carried on and we knew we had to start looking for a building, as our capacity was growing and we were having to turn down children due to limited space. We decided to enlist the help of the Business Advisor from the City Council, who mentioned at one of our meetings that the Council may be putting out some of their buildings for tender.

We decided to move with God's timing after an agreed deal fell through on a seemingly well-located building. It was a move worth-the-while, as God began to move gloriously in our lives. Whilst we were looking for a place to accommodate our rapid expansion, we had submitted a request to the Manchester City Council Corporate Property department to check if they had any property for sale. They informed us that they did not have any property suitable for a nursery, but if anything cropped up they would let us know. When the Manchester Council decided to put up some of their nurseries for tender, we were informed by the dept. On the 28th of April in 2013, as I sat in a Sunday service, the word of the Lord came to me regarding the acquisition of the buildings for the proposed nursery. God said that **He would not only give us one nursery building, but that he would give us two before the end of 2013, and He would also add a third one in the early part of 2014. He further said that he would do it after the order of my foremost mentor, who presently has two Universities and is planning for a third one.** I heard those words as a man will hear his friends and I told them to my wife. I also shared it with two of my friends. One of them recently confessed that at the time, he thought, 'This brother has gone too far now.' But when God is with and for you, he will tell you things that are above your natural comprehension and expect you to believe it!

On the strength of His words, we decided as an act of faith to put in a bid knowing that we are well favoured of God. The tough part was that we had to tender for three instead of one. It wasn't easy, but we believed God. We had never written a tender in our lives, but we decided we were going to write this by ourselves and we did. We submitted and left it there. We were pleasantly surprised when we were advised that we had successfully crossed the first hurdle, which meant we have been shortlisted onto the Council's framework. Now we had to go through a second phase, which would be tendering for individual properties in areas we desired, property viewing, and pricing. This is something I had never done before and commercial property price comparison is quite a difficult task. Again, I told God to show me what to bid and he did. I slept and saw a figure. As I deliberated with the accountants and my wife, I said 'I will go with the figure God had shown me' and that was it. I stuck with the figure and it has never been a struggle to pay.

The day we went to view the first property, I was so scared when I got inside that I couldn't finish the viewing. The enormity of what we were about to take on became too apparent. I saw the bills, I saw the staff salary, I saw the business rates and maintenance cost. Everything that the devil could put in front of me to make me backtrack was placed in front of me that day. I was being moved by what I was seeing and not the Word of God. It was mind-boggling. I knew instinctively that I needed to leave the viewing and be with God. I told my wife I needed to be in church to seek God again. I drove back straight to church and as I was contemplating what song to 'enter his gate' with (Ps 100:4), his soothing words came to me from **Isaiah 66:8-9 (NLT)** and I could never forget it. **He said: '8 "Who has heard of such a thing? Who has seen such things? Can a land [a]be born in one day? Or can a nation be brought forth in a moment? As soon as Zion was in labor, she also brought forth her sons. 9 "Shall I bring to the moment of birth and not give delivery?" says the Lord. "Or shall I who gives delivery shut the womb?" says your God.'** That was it for me. If God spoke about it, He has a completion agenda. It is God's power that will bring it to pass not mine. I went back home with a renewed take-over vigour.

As the Lord had said, we were offered one property in August 2013, which opened in September 2013. Another in December 2013, which was operational in January 2014, and the third in January 2014, which became operational in March 2014. God had proved himself and confirmed His words. We have since added another nursery, which goes to show the Might of God. We presently have approximately 60 staff on our payroll and not once have we had to think twice about paying their salaries or where it is going to come from. From God saying "give me all you have" in November 2002, to an amazing financially free position, I can say that

God can move anyone from 'Zero to Abundance' in a twinkle of an eye. However, having close partnership with God & submission, trust in His word; with diligence and obedience are important keys to actualisation of His plans. If God asks you for your stuff, be sure it is your time for a miracle. I guess those guys who said I would spend all my life in UK as a poor man, are all languishing in jail right now for fraud. God shows no favouritism and it does not matter which land you live or come from. 'If God SENDS you, God will FEND for you! Shalom

-    Olusola Andrew Omole

## About the Author – Olusola Andrew Omole

Andrew was born in Newcastle, UK but spent most of his teenage and young adult life in Africa where he learnt valuable lessons in business. As a young man, he worked at his father's agricultural plantation. It was there he cut his teeth in business management and leadership. At harvest times, he would have at least 5 to 10 manual labour to support. He was responsible for daily operations, attendance of the labour force, transportation, and packaging. This fired up his desire for excellence and to support others to become their best in life. It was the start of his entrepreneurial journey.

From earning £3.50 an hour working in a shop, Andrew presently leads a staff team of 55 who rely heavily on his visionary leadership.

He is the CEO of WMB Childcare Ltd, a company that supports parents and guardians to lay solid early years foundation for their children. He is a serial entrepreneur, straight-talking mentor, a life coach and trainer. He is a Ziglar Certified Legacy Trainer having been adopted into the Ziglar family.

When he's not working on the business, Andrew serves at his local church under the spiritual leadership of his mentor. He served as the Pastoral Oversight for the Youth and Teenage arm of the church for a couple of years leading a strong group of young individuals and university students in the path of finding purpose and fulfilment.

Andrew likes writing in his spare time. He has been known to spend a large amount of his time studying his favourite all-time book, the Bible. Andrew is married to ever-smiling Folake and has two great children.

Olusola Andrew Omole
Phone No: 447737930793
FB Pages:
@olusola.omole
@towardsyoursignificance
Email - andrew@towards-your-significance.com

"When God is with and for you,
he will tell you things that are above your natural
comprehension and expect you to believe it!"
-    Olusola Andrew Omole

# Chapter 6 – From Zero to Abundance

Pursuing Success, Stories That Inspire

# EPILOGUE

Throughout my life, I have always felt a bigger and better purpose for my life, but I have not always been in pursuit of it, mostly because I have been my own biggest obstacle. I was often distracted by my current comfort zones through my current routines. They kept me from stepping into my full potential and kept me as a prisoner to my routines. I knew that I wanted to "pursue success," I was just not focused enough to see it or empowered enough to make a change.

After years of very strong feelings that God had something better for me, I only took action to start changing my life, when I chose to have faith and act on God's plan for me. I knew this was the only way to fix my life.

Through His grace, I am a new man. I understand my purpose and I am full of life. I can see Him clearly, and I am stronger than ever.

Regarding success, I have always felt that my purpose was to help others through the gift of speaking. I have always dreamed of becoming a motivational/inspirational speaker, but for the largest part of my life, I only considered this a dream.
Who was I to be a speaker?
What credentials or gifts did I have?
These were negative thoughts that I burdened myself with.

So, who am I?
I am a son of our King.
I know Him and He knows me.

Today, all because of Him, and through my obedience to decide, take action and have faith, I am living my life's dream. I am pursuing my life's goal, and most importantly, my life's purpose to help others build their lives.

Believe in God and His plan for your life. Have faith and take action. You too can make all of your dreams come true because you are also the son or daughter of the same King!

Now Go Forth and Make YOUR Life Exceptional!

- **Mike Rodriguez**

## About Mike Rodriguez

Mike Rodriguez is CEO of Mike Rodriguez International, a professional speaking and training firm. Besides being a Best-Selling author, he is a world-renowned motivator and a leadership and sales expert. Mike also owns a publishing company and still manages to spend quality time with his wife and their five daughters. He is a former showcase speaker with the world-famous Zig Ziglar Corporation and was selected as their featured speaker for the 2015 Ziglar U.S. Tour. Mike has also co-hosted training alongside the legendary Tom Hopkins.

Mike delivers performance-based seminars and trainings and has authored several books which have been promoted by Barnes & Noble. He has been featured on CBS, U.S. News & World Report, Fast Company, and Success Magazine. He has lectured at Baylor University, UNT, and K-State Research. His clients include names like Hilton, McDonald's Corporation, and the Federal Government. As a sales expert, Mike has trained thousands.

Everyone faces challenges; Mike believes that through faith and action, you can overcome the challenges in your life to attain your goals and become who you truly want to be.

Throughout his career, Mike has built productivity-driven training programs and managed multi-million dollar quotas. He has experience delivering powerful messages and creating personal development strategies for new and tenured companies and teams across many industries.

Mike has been happily married since 1991 to Bonnie, the love of his life. He believes if you have the right attitude and the right faith, you can have the right kind of success, regardless of the type of industry that you are in.

Pursuing Success, Stories That Inspire

As a world-renowned speaker,
Mike has experience working with people
from all walks of life.

You can schedule Mike Rodriguez
to speak or train at your next event.
Go to:
www.MikeRodriguezInternational.com

**Audio Course available by Mike Rodriguez in partnership with Nightingale Conant**

**The Power of Breaking Routines**

**Other books available by Mike Rodriguez:**

Finding Your WHY

8 Keys to Exceptional Selling

Break Your Routines to Fix Your Life

Lion Leadership

Think BIG Motivational Quotes

Walking with Faith

Life Builders

Pursuing Success, Stories That Inspire

## Disclaimer & Copyright Information

References for Shane Adamson's Chapter

Kids Internet Humor Source Internet:
www-personal.umich.edu/~bpl/kids.html

Change Yourself, Change Your Marriage, Douglas Abbot, 2004
Journal of Marriage and Family, Brigham Young University

Blanket Stepping Ceremony, Anasazi Wilderness Therapy
Program, Phoenix Arizona

*"I can do ALL THINGS through Christ*
*who strengthens me."*
*Philippians 4:13*

NOTES

## NOTES

# NOTES

CPSIA information can be obtained
at www.ICGtesting.com
Printed in the USA
LVOW11s1317041216
515739LV00002B/103/P